Legends *of* Animation

Walt
Disney

Legends of Animation

Tex Avery:
Hollywood's Master of Screwball Cartoons

Walt Disney:
The Mouse that Roared

Matt Groening:
From Spitballs to Springfield

William Hanna and Joseph Barbera:
The Sultans of Saturday Morning

Legends *of* Animation

Walt
Disney

The Mouse that Roared

Jeff Lenburg

CHELSEA HOUSE
An Infobase Learning Company

Walt Disney: The Mouse that Roared

Chelsea House
An Infobase Learning Company
132 West 31st Street
New York NY 10001

Library of Congress Cataloging-in-Publication Data
Lenburg, Jeff.
  Walt Disney : the mouse that roared / Jeff Lenburg. — 1st ed.
      p. cm. — (Legends of animation)
  Includes bibliographical references and index.
  ISBN-13: 978-1-60413-836-8 (hardcover : alk. paper)
  ISBN-10: 1-60413-836-X (hardcover : alk. paper) 1. Disney, Walt, 1901-1966—
Juvenile literature. 2. Animators—United States—Biography—Juvenile literature.
I. Disney, Walt, 1901-1966. II. Title. III. Series.
  NC1766.U52D54533 2011
  791.43092—dc22
  [B]   2010051580

Chelsea House books are available at special discounts when purchased in bulk quantities for businesses, associations, institutions, or sales promotions. Please call our Special Sales Department in New York at (212) 967-8800 or (800) 322-8755.

You can find Chelsea House on the World Wide Web at
http://www.infobaselearning.com

Text design by Kerry Casey
Cover design by Takeshi Takahashi
Composition by EJB Publishing Services
Cover printed by Yurchak Printing, Landisville, Pa.
Book printed and bound by Yurchak Printing, Landisville, Pa.
Date printed: May 2011

Printed in the United States of America

10 9 8 7 6 5 4 3 2 1

This book is printed on acid-free paper.

All links and Web addresses were checked and verified to be correct at the time of publication. Because of the dynamic nature of the Web, some addresses and links may have changed since publication and may no longer be valid.

To my literal "other half" (and "full man"),
my twin brother, Greg, with love

CONTENTS

ACKNOWLEDGMENTS

Special thanks to David R. Smith of the Walt Disney Studios Archives for his kind and generous assistance in providing numerous details, answers, and pieces of information on Disney animation in chronicling previous histories and that proved helpful to the biographer.

Many thanks to the Margaret Herrick Library of the Academy of Motion Picture Arts and Sciences; the Archives of Performing Arts and the Regional History Collections at the University of Southern California; the *Los Angeles Times* Photographic Archive of the University of California, Los Angeles Library; Arizona State University West, Fletcher Library; Associated Press, and United Press International for the use of research; oral histories; transcripts; books; newspaper, magazine and trade articles; photographs; and other documents vital to the success of this project.

My deepest gratitude to the following publications—the *Anaheim Bulletin*, *Los Angeles Daily News*, *Los Angeles Times*, *Hollywood Reporter*, *The Film Daily*, *Motion Picture Herald*, *Motion Picture News*, *The Moving Picture World*, *Variety*, *Film Comment*, *Funnyworld*, *Griffithiana*, *Journal of Popular Culture*, and *Mindrot*—for their extensive coverage of the subject's films and career that were of great value in researching and writing this biography.

Finally, to the legendary Walt Disney, thank you for your inspiration and for instilling in this former Disneyland cast member and generations of followers the common belief that if you follow your heart, dreams will come true.

An Innovator in the Making

Four theme parks in Anaheim, Orlando, Tokyo, and France today bear his name, along with everything from a major motion picture studio, to a television production arm, to a distribution company, to a home video division, to an animation studio. He was a father figure to millions of baby boomers weaned on serials and cartoons of his making. He was an American original who took the animated film to new levels of artistic and technical achievement, made a massive contribution to the folklore of the world, and created a now multibillion dollar industry. Known for his innovative and pioneering spirit, he is remembered for countless creations, most of all, his beloved Mickey Mouse, which have brought laughter and enjoyment to fans around the world. While other legendary filmmakers have come and gone, he remains one of the most important and honored producers and animators of 20th-century animation and a man whose creative vision is still celebrated today. He is the man behind the mouse that roared and much more. He is none other than Walt Disney.

Born in the upper bedroom of their Tripp Avenue house in Chicago, Illinois, on December 5, 1901, to his father, Elias, an Irish-Canadian, and mother, the former Flora Call, of German-American descent, Walter Elias Disney was the fourth son of five children after brothers

Herbert, Raymond, and Roy, and followed by a younger sister, the only girl, Ruth. The third son, Roy, who would later become a business partner and integral part of Walt's success in animation, was eight years old at the time of Walt's birth.

Raised in a lower middle-class household of hard work and tight purse strings, Walt's father was a trained carpenter who found work at the World's Columbian Exposition after moving to Chicago in 1893. He went on to become a contractor, building houses and reselling them, while his mother, a patient woman and former schoolteacher, supported her husband's numerous business pursuits. Walt was named after his father and the St. Paul Congregational Church minister, Walter Robinson Parr, who baptized him in June 1902.

A stiff-backed socialist, Elias was a highly religious man and old-fashioned martinet who was strict, honest, and decent, never drank, and rarely smoked. He was also quick tempered and impatient, however, and a strict disciplinarian whom his children feared. Speaking in a thick Irish brogue, he "had a peculiar way of talking" that often left young Walt confused. As Walt later revealed, "He'd get mad at me and call me a little scud. He says, 'You little scud, I'll take a gad to you,' and I found out later when I was digging into Irish lore and things, that a scud was equivalent to a little squirt . . . and a gad is something they used to sort of flail, you know, they used to beat the grain with it."

Throughout Walt's childhood, Elias displayed an entrepreneurial spirit. He was hell-bent on being successful in his own business and typically moved his family with him.

In April 1906, seeking "a more wholesome country life" for his children, free of the crime and corruption of Chicago, Elias moved them to Marceline, Missouri, a small town of about 2,500 residents. That March, for $3,000 he bought a 40-acre farm with a two-story house and a big yard—originally owned by a Civil War veteran—that would become their new family home. A month later, he purchased the adjoining tract of five acres for an additional $450.

In those days, residents of this former frontier town enjoyed direct transportation by train. In 1886, the Atchison, Topeka and Santa Fe Railroad Company established direct service to Marceline between

Immortalized in bronze in 1993, Walt and Mickey Mouse stand in front of Sleeping Beauty Castle at Disneyland greeting guests who visit his famed theme park.

Chicago and Kansas City. Flora, Roy, Walt, and Ruth arrived separately ahead of Elias and Herbert and Raymond. Walt was only four years old at the time. After arriving, their neighbor, Mr. Coffman, drove them out to their new farm by horse-drawn wagon.

The sprawling farm was more than Walt ever imagined, with "a beautiful front yard with lots of weeping willow trees" and abundant apple, peach, and plum orchards, fields of grain, and home to dozens of animals—hogs, chickens, horses, and cows. Living there left a lasting impression on him. As he warmly remembered, "It had two orchards, one called the old and one called the new. We had every kind of apple growing in that orchard. We had what we called Wolf River apples. They were that big . . . People came from miles around to see our orchard. To see these big things."

Walt developed a deep love of nature, later embodied in his film work. Often he gazed in wonderment out his window at the natural beauty, able to recall every detail later as an adult. He grew attached to the blissful environment, and to a horse named Charlie, whom he enjoyed riding. "All of us kids would climb on old Charlie's back, and he would head straight for the apple orchard and a tree with very low branches," he recalled. "Then we'd all have to scramble off Charlie's back pretty fast." Walt's exploits on horseback became legendary as he frequently ended up in the pond.

Walt had one unhappy encounter on the farm with an owl. The owl, half-blinded by daylight, was sitting on a low branch of a tree when he crept up behind it to grab it. The screeching owl whirled on him and "scared me to death." In his moment of terror, he stomped on the owl and killed it, something he later regretted. "I've never forgotten that poor bird," Walt said, "and maybe that has something to do with my liking for animals."

In the fall of 1908, Elias's strict disciplinarian standards resulted in Herbert and Raymond sneaking out the window of their first-floor bedroom one night and going back to Chicago and later Kansas City to work as clerks. The loss of his two oldest sons was a tremendous blow to Elias, dashing any hopes of turning the 45 acres of prairie land into a prosperous working farm.

Despite any misgivings they had privately, Walt and Roy both called their father "the kindest fellow" who "thought of nothing but his family" and loved people. As for facing his father's wrath, Walt "got off easy," as Elias was usually too worn-out after chasing his other brothers to scold him.

In the fall of 1909, Walt and his sister Ruth started attending the year-old Park School. Unlike most children his age, he was an old soul at heart who identified more with older adults. Often he palled around with his neighbors, both in their 70s, a retired doctor, Leighton "Doc" I. Sherwood, and "Grandpa" E. H. Taylor, and with his widowed grandmother, Mary Richardson Disney, Elias's mother, a frequent family visitor.

DRAWING ATTENTION

At age seven, Walt exhibited his first interests in drawing. Mr. Sherwood paid him a "nickel or something" to draw a picture of his fine stallion on his homemade easel, praising his drawing "to my great delight," as Walt later recalled. Aunt Margaret Disney, the wife of Elias's brother, Robert, was equally encouraging. She bought him pads of paper and crayons, inundated him with art books, and heaped on the praise. He responded by producing more drawings, most of which Sherwood snapped up. In an artful display, Walt also covered the family's two-story farmhouse with animal "figures painted with tar" used to seal a barrel that caught rainwater.

Walt quickly learned that nothing in life is ever permanent. Elias became severely ill with typhoid fever and then pneumonia, forcing him to sell the family farm due to financial hardship. During the cold of winter, he auctioned off the stock. Then, on November 28, 1910, the farm sold, and Elias rented a house downtown so Roy, Walt, and Ruth could finish the school year.

On May 17, 1911, Elias moved the whole family to Kansas City, again renting a house. That September, Walt attended nearby Benton Grammar School, where he was required by the school system to repeat second grade and his teachers further encouraged him in his artistic pursuits. Almost every child who came from another school had trouble, but his second-grade teacher, Ethel Fisher, recalled to a friend, "Walt could draw; he was talented." When Ruth fell ill, he designed his first flip book for her, a series of hand-drawn figures that moved in sequence, his first entry in the world of animation.

Walt displayed minimal interest in his class work. He had a short attention span and his reading level was perfunctory. Flora homeschooled her young son by reading the classic adventures of the century's greatest storytellers—Mark Twain, Horatio Alger, Robert Louis Stevenson, Sir Walter Scott, and Charles Dickens.

During the next 12 years, Walt would experience many significant events that forever defined his life. Elias, at age 51, bought a newspaper distributorship for the morning *Kansas City Times* and evening and Sunday *Kansas City Star* newspapers for $2,100 and put both Roy and Walt to work delivering newspapers with him. The work itself was grueling and taught them the value of hard work. Typically rising at 3:30 every morning, Walt would help his father claim the newspapers from the delivery truck an hour later. For six years, during sweltering hot summers and bitterly cold winters, they delivered the morning *Times* to nearly 700 customers and evening and Sunday *Star* to more than 600 customers, missing only four weeks of work due to illness.

Elias was a taskmaster. He forbade them from riding bicycles and throwing newspapers on customers' porches or yard, insisting they carry the papers to the front door instead. As Walt once said, "I still have nightmares about it, missing a customer along their route and waking up sweating and thinking, 'I'll have to rush back and leave a paper before Dad finds out.'"

Occasionally Walt strayed from his backbreaking and character-building work. A child at heart, he would pause on verandas of rich homes on his route to play with borrowed toys. "I'll never forget. . . . I sat there in the early dawn eating a box of candy and racing an electric train left behind," he said. "It was fifteen minutes of stolen delight and I've never been able to recapture that moment of enchantment."

The following summer, Walt, now 10, got his second taste of operating a business. He and a childhood friend set up a pop stand to sell drinks to passersby, but "it ran about three weeks and we drank up all the profits."

Roy kept up his interest in the newspaper route until graduating from Manual Training High School in 1912. Afterwards, he worked on his uncle's farm. Then he accepted a job at Kansas City's First National Bank, where he became "a steady, conscientious worker," while Walt still delivered newspapers with Elias until after 1917.

Throughout it all, Walt demonstrated an avid interest in drawing. He drew cartoons for a local barber, Bert Hudson, owner of the Benton Barber Shop—caricatures of "all the critters that hung out"—in exchange for free haircuts.

Occasionally, Walt's drawing got him in trouble. When he was seventh grade, the principal J. M. Cottinghman, who used to roam from room to room, reprimanded him. Instead of studying geography in class, Walt was slouched in his chair drawing cartoons behind his big geography book. Cottingham told him, "Young man, you'll never amount to anything."

Walt was a friendly boy, but did not have many close companions. He never socialized much. While most students stuck around after school to play basketball, he was more involved in drawing his cartoons.

During his school days, however, Walt developed into "quite a ham." He said, "I loved this drawing business but everything was a means to an end." At school, he produced his own stage plays, making his own scenery; staging, directing and acting in them; and making other kids laugh. At home, Walt also did anything to attract attention, performing assorted magic tricks that sent his mother Flora into fits of laughter.

To that end, Walt competed in amateur vaudeville. With Kansas City becoming a hive of Chaplin-impersonation contests in 1913, he entered these contests wearing a black wig made out of old hemp (later out of crepe) that smelled of creosote. Chuckling, he once noted, "I'd get in line with a half dozen guys. I'd ad lib and play with my cane and gloves. Sometimes I'd win $5, sometimes $2.50, sometimes just get car fare." Walt often performed skits on amateur nights at local theaters as

Walt admires caricatures of many of his studio's famous creations, beginning with Mickey Mouse. *Courtesy: Academy of Motion Picture Arts and Sciences Library. © Walt Disney Productions.*

well with his neighbor Walter Pfeiffer, with Walt's Chaplin called "the second-best" in Kansas City.

After purchasing a small new house in September 1914, at 3028 Bellefontaine Avenue for his family, Elias, besides managing the newspaper route, started importing butter and eggs from a dairy in Marceline to sell to his customers to make ends meet, and enlisted Walt to help him. "I was working all the time," Walt later said.

FINDING HIS WAY

In 1915, at age 14, Walt became serious about his craft. He talked his father into letting him take children's art classes for two winters, three nights a week in Kansas City, sponsored by the Fine Arts Institute. His home life, however, remained in flux. Two years later, Elias moved himself, Flora, and Ruth back to Chicago, after selling the newspaper route to become part owner of a jelly factory, the O-Zell Company, after Walt and Ruth graduated from seventh grade that June. Walt stayed to work the route for its new owner, living with Roy, older brother Herbert, and Herbert's wife and baby daughter.

For two summers, Roy worked for the Fred Harvey Company as a vendor of candy, fruit, and soft drinks—called "a news butcher"—on the Santa Fe trains chugging through Kansas City. Walt did not continue to deliver newspapers for much longer. Then 15, he lied about his age to work with Roy as a news butcher, selling concessions for the Van Noy Interstate Company, which operated concessions on many railroads throughout the country. For the first time, Walt went into business without being under the strict control of his father. He rode different trains on the Missouri Pacific to surrounding states. Despite many disappointments to come, including customers taking advantage of his naïveté by playing "cruel jokes" and stealing empty soda bottles from him, cutting into his profits, he considered the job "a very exciting thing."

With mounting indebtedness to his employer, however, by the end of the summer, Walt left his job and Kansas City. He moved to Chicago to join his parents, who were renting a flat on the west side. There, Walt enrolled in eighth grade at McKinley High School. As before, he worked for his father, this time at the jelly factory, washing bottles and crushing apples, and as a pistol-packing night watchman after he turned 16.

Walt never lost sight of his love of drawing, however. To hone his craft, he attended classes three nights a week at the Chicago Academy of Fine Arts, while demonstrating his talent by day at McKinley High, rendering crudely drawn cartoons for its monthly magazine, *The Voice*, whose characters were reminiscent of those in George McManus's comic-strip *Bringing Up Father*.

By July 1918, after working for Elias, Walt held down two jobs at once—as a mail sorter and substitute carrier for the Chicago Post Office. He worked from the early morning to mid-afternoon, taking on other work at the post office after his shift was over before going to the South Side to work as a gate man loading trains during rush hour. Still under-age, he wore his father's clothes to appear older, fibbed about his age, and the post office hired him. Working as hard as he did, Walt never regretted one moment, saying, "I have no recollection of ever being unhappy in my life. I look back and I worked from way back there and I was happy all the time."

In the meantime, in June 1917, Roy joined the Navy following the outbreak of World War I. After seeing his brother in uniform on his way to the Great Lakes Naval Training Station that fall, Walt wanted to sign up but was too young—he would be 16 that December.

Walt never gave up the dream. Struggling through high school, that summer while still working at the Chicago Post Office, he signed up through the Red Cross to become a driver for the American Ambulance Corps. To obtain a passport, necessary to travel to Europe, he had to be 17. On the affidavit, Walt falsified his year of birth as 1900 instead of 1901, to appear the legal age. Still, he required the signature of both parents. Elias refused, but Flora, knowing how important this was, signed the affidavit for both of them.

Shortly thereafter, Walt became sick during the great flu epidemic that swept the country in 1918. Thus, his travels to Europe to fulfill his obligations were delayed. By the time he was well and joined the Red Cross unit in France, the war had ended that December. He spent almost the next year driving in the motor pool to evacuate hospitals overseas before returning to Chicago in the fall of 1919. Walt was treated no differently than as a news butcher by his fellow compatriots. On his 17th birthday, they celebrated with him at a French bar by enjoying numerous libations and having him foot the bill. Walt took such jesting in stride, but got even. He became a successful craps player, winning $500 from others in his unit.

Walt came back to the States determined to become an artist. During his time overseas, he managed to find time to draw and submitted some of his cartoons to different humor magazines including *Life* and *Judge*. Despite having his work rejected, he remained undeterred and was paid by guys in his unit for the assorted caricatures he drew for them.

Back home, Walt was offered a job at his father's jelly factory for $25 a week, but he was done doing "physically demanding work." After Roy was discharged in February 1919 and took a job as a bank teller in Kansas City, Walt followed to live with Roy, Herbert, and Herbert's wife and daughter in the old family home.

The seeds, however, for Walt's future had been planted. His love for drawing was about to start him on a whole new trek toward his destiny.

2

The Unrepentant Animator

Deciding to become a successful cartoonist, Walt applied for a job at the *Kansas City Star*, the same newspaper he delivered for many years with Elias and Roy. Working as a delivery boy, he hung around the art department persistently peddling his talent to the staff cartoonists, seeking a staff job but to no avail. As he later said, ". . . I guess fate was against letting me be a successful cartoonist . . . I wondered if I could ever reach the top."

Unwavering in his determination, in October 1919, Walt landed work as an apprentice for Pesmen-Rubin Commercial Art Studio, a local business, after showing "corny" samples of the work he had done in France to Louis A. Pesmen and Bill Rubin, with his salary to be determined later. Walt worked diligently that first week. Rubin liked what he saw and offered him $50 a month. Walt was delighted; it was the first time he had ever been paid professionally to draw.

Working alongside Walt was fellow Kansas Cityan and budding cartoonist born to Dutch-American parents, Ubbe Ert Iwwerks, who later shortened his first name to "Ub" and last name to "Iwerks" in the late-1920s and would become an important collaborator in Walt's career. Despite their obvious personality differences—Walt, an outgoing prankster, and Ub, quiet and reserved—they became fast friends as Walt

spent his time drawing chickens, cows, and eggs for farm paper advertisements. Living on the family farm in Marceline was never far from his
mind. That "old farm certainly made an impression on me," Walt said.
"I don't know a lot about farming, but when I see a drawing of a pig or
duck or a rooster I know immediately if it has the right feeling. And I
know it because of what I learned during those days on the farm."

Walt enjoyed the work, but after he illustrated catalogs that fall,
Pesmen-Rubin laid him off after six weeks on the job, along with Iwerks
and others. Nonetheless, he considered his time there worthwhile,
learning numerous "tricks of the commercial [art] business."

In the interim, Walt worked as a mail carrier for the Kansas City
Post Office during the Christmas rush while seeking another commercial art job. In early January 1920, Iwerks, then supporting his mother,
contacted Walt and after talking, Walt suggested, "Let's go into business." Using half of the $500 he had saved from his time overseas, they
formed their own commercial art studio, Iwerks-Disney Commercial
Artists (originally considering calling themselves Disney-Iwerks, but
Walt feared it sounded too much like an eyewear factory). The first
month, they grossed a respectable $135, but most days were a struggle.

To remain solvent, Walt sought other work while Iwerks ran their
business. On January 20, 1920, he saw an ad in *The Kansas City Star*
that read: "Artist, Cartoon and Wash Drawings, First Class Man Wanted,
Steady, Kansas City Slide Company." He answered the ad and was hired
by A. V. ("Verne") Cauger, president of the company. He paid Walt $40
a week, far more than he had ever earned previously. As a result of his
departure, his and Iwerks's new enterprise did not last long. While an
entrepreneur like his father, Walt lacked the strong business sense of his
brother Roy, who was much savvier in the areas of business and finance.
Consequently, they closed their business after only a couple of months.
By March, Iwerks joined Walt after he persuaded the owners to hire
him. By then, the company had moved and was renamed the Kansas
City Film Ad Company.

Learning the basics of animation, Walt and Iwerks produced primi-
tively animated one-minute advertising films, doing little actual drawing and relying on human and animal figures made out of paper-cut

Early 1920s advertisement from Walt Disney's days as a cartoonist in Kansas City.

animation, shown at local movie houses. Like television commercials of today, the films were built around advertising campaign slogans such as "Put your winter coal in early" and "Get your Fedora blocked for the winter." Recalling their simplistic filmic ads, Walt once described, "There was one little one I did. . .you had to think up little gags, little catch things, you know. So I had this spanking, shining car drive in and I had a character on the street. He hailed the driver and he says, 'Hi, old top, new car?' and the guy in the car says, 'No, old car, new top.' Then we'd go into the pitch of where to get them renewed."

At this time, cartoon animation had become a popular form of entertainment in movie theaters across the country, featuring weekly installments of silent cartoon shorts. Back then, New York was known as "the hub of animation," where many such films—Bud Fisher's *Mutt and Jeff*, Max and Dave Fleischer's *Out of the Inkwell*, George Herriman's *Krazy Kat*, Pat Sullivan's *Felix the Cat*, and others—were produced by studios run by pioneer animators and cartoonists. After noticing greater realism and movement achieved in popular animated cartoons of the day and becoming growingly dissatisfied with the crude animation methods he was using, Walt was determined to learn more about the mechanics of cartoon animation to make his work better.

Walt quickly gained a better understanding of the process and developed his own system after reading one book that had a profound impact on him: Edwin G. Lutz's *Animated Cartoons: How They Are Made, Their Origin and Development*, published in February 1920. After eagerly poring over every page of this simple handbook, the resourceful 18-year-old applied innovations from Lutz's book in his drawings at work, showing marked improvement in their realism and receiving praise from his employer. He also injected gags into the material copywriters of the film ads gave him, using "tricks that they hadn't done." At first his boss, Cauger, was impressed by Walt taking the extra initiative. In time, however, the incremental changes he made backfired, with Cauger labeling him a disruptive influence and "too inquisitive." Walt dismissed the misunderstanding, saying, "he [Cauger] was kind of sore at me, because I think he felt the boss paid me too much." Walt was paid more than any of the other artists—$10 extra a week, except for Iwerks, who earned five dollars less a week than the others.

Thereafter, his superiors looked upon everything Walt suggested with growing suspicion. Still desiring to do more, he borrowed an unused company camera and rigged up his own studio in the garage that his father had built at their home on Bellefontaine Street in mid-1920 after returning to Kansas City with Flora and retiring after selling his interests in the jelly factory. Working again as a carpenter, he built the garage for Walt to earn some extra money, thereafter charging Walt five dollars a month rent. (Roy recalls never seeing any money actually change hands between them.)

At night, Walt began doing experimental animation in his spare time in his cartoon shop, using the movie camera he borrowed. He

subsequently produced an editorial cartoon featuring caricature drawings and himself in live-action at the beginning as a lightning-fast sketch
artist doing blue-penciled drawings and then inking and photographing
them in sequence. In the same film, he used cutout animation to edi-
torialize the periodic scandals of the Kansas City police department in
another segment, called "Kansas City's Spring Cleanup." Walt titled his
animation reel *Newman Laugh-O-grams*, borrowing the name of Kansas
City's famed Newman Theatre, to sell the owner of the theater on buying it and making it a regular feature.

Walt arranged to show the 300-foot cartoon to Milton Feld, the
manager of the Newman Theatre Company, which owned three movie
houses in Kansas City. In the darkened theater, he sat nervously behind
Feld as he screened the film, wondering if he would like it. After watching the film, Feld snapped his head around and said, "I like it, kid. Is it
expensive?"

Quickly calculating his expenses, Walt blurted, "No sir; I can make
it for 30 cents a foot."

Feld replied, "It's a deal. I'll buy all you can make."

Still learning the business, Walt walked out of the theater exuber-
ant over his triumph until realizing the deal he made was not so great
after all. The 30 cents a foot was his *actual* cost. As a result, he would
make the films for no profit. It would not be the last instance illustrat-
ing Walt's naïveté for business and how he was best to let others handle
his affairs.

Nonetheless, Walt forged ahead producing the series. On March
20, 1921, he premiered his first *Newman Laugh-O-gram* opposite the
silent feature *Mamma's Affair*, starring actress Constance Talmadge. He
went on to produce 12 more one-minute cartoons satirizing topics of
interest to Kansas City audiences, all shown locally, and for someone so
new to animation, he displayed surprising skill in the films ads, drawing
them with lightning speed.

STRIKING OUT ON HIS OWN

Becoming locally famous, Walt, now making $60 a week at the Film Ad
Company, saved enough money to buy a used Universal camera and

rent his own shop downtown to animate his films at night. He also advertised in the local paper to recruit other animators to "learn the cartoon business" to work with him. Around this time, he befriended a young artist who ultimately replaced him: Fred Harman, the younger brother of animator Hugh Harman, who became one of Walt's first animators. Walt went into partnership with Fred Harman to produce their own animated cartoons, "secretly" setting up Kaycee Studios to try to become "the next Paul Terry." Terry was a pioneer New York animator who had enjoyed success producing a series of animated *Aesop's Film Fables*, first released to theaters in June 1921. The partnership between Walt and Harman fizzled, however. It ended a few months later after they got behind in their rent. This was after Walt purchased a second Model T Ford Coupe that was repossessed.

By that July, Walt was left to fend for himself. His brother Herbert and his family pulled up stakes and moved to Portland, Oregon, with Elias, Flora, and Ruth following them by train that November. Complicating matters, that fall, Roy fell ill with tuberculosis. He was moved out of state to a series of Veterans Administration–run sanatoriums in sunnier and drier climates—in New Mexico, Arizona, and then southern California—to recuperate. For injuries sustained as a veteran of World War I, he received disability compensation of $85 a month.

For the first time Walt was without the support of his family close by. After new owners moved into the Bellefontaine house, he moved to a rooming house. By then his enterprise had outgrown the garage, so he also rented a small shop nearby for his cartoon business.

In May 1922, at age 20, Walt left the Film Ad Company and incorporated his own studio, Laugh-O-gram Films Inc., retaining the series' original name. As a young entrepreneur, he issued 300 shares of stock through his corporation valued at $50 a share to attract investors, selling a 51 percent stake in his company. With $15,000 from investors, he set up shop on the second floor of the McConahy Building on 1127 East 31st Street in downtown Kansas City, purchasing new equipment to fill the five-room suite. Walt hired five animators—Hugh Harman, Rudolf Ising, Carman Griffin "Max" Maxwell, Lorey Tague, and Otto Walliman—plus a business manager, inker and painter, salesman, and secretary as his staff. A month later, a weakened Roy, still feeling the effects of tuberculosis, joined him to work on the production, only with his illness forcing him to move into an out-of-state sanitarium to recover, and a new sales manager, Leslie Mace, to arrange distribution.

Walt quickly completed his first fully animated, yet-to-be-released cartoon, *Little Red Riding Hood*. In June 1922, he had announced plans to produce a new series—releasing one film every two weeks—of 12 updated versions of popular fairy tales, called *Laugh-O-grams*. In many respects, he modeled them after Paul Terry's modernized *Aesop's Fables* that he had once studied. M. J. Winkler distributed the series, paying Walt $1,500 per reel. Walt turned a profit on the first one that cost him only $750 to produce. His first six-minute, black-and-white silent cartoon—and the last produced in his family's garage—released to theaters on July 29 of that year was the aforementioned *Little Red Riding Hood*.

Though roughly drawn, *Little Red Riding Hood* represented a real triumph as Walt's first widely distributed film. It also marked his first celluloid animated production in which the drawings were traced and inked on celluloid sheets, painted and aligned with the cels over background drawings, and then photographed in sequence, unlike others in the series that were mostly comprised of photographed inked lines on paper and occasional cel animation.

Walt was true to his word, producing additional modernized fairy tales: in August, *The Four Musicians of Bremen*; in early September, *Jack and the Beanstalk*; and in early October, *Goldie Locks and the Three Bears*. Meanwhile, that September, he contracted another company, the Pictorial Clubs, to distribute his films to schools and churches, giving him $100 along with a note promising $11,000 for six cartoons altogether. In accepting the deal, Walt made the same mistake of underselling his films at cost, as he had done before. No doubt that is why he eventually turned business operations over to Roy, whom he implicitly trusted, freeing him to focus more on the creative end of the business.

That November, with limited capital, Walt resumed production of a second series of short joke reels begun that spring, called *Lafflets*. The one-minute live-action/animated films, some using clay modeling and matchstick animation, were usually based on jokes from *Judge* and *Life* magazines. The jerky and simply produced films were originally done by Walt's animators for "fun" and to "experiment." But given their built-in novelty appeal and how quickly they could be made, he looked upon them as another source of income to possibly "tide his company over."

Despite the success of the first four *Laugh-O-grams*, producing the rest of the series was rough sledding. By October, while producing the fifth, *Puss in Boots*, Walt's young studio fell into trouble. Any assets he had had vanished, and he was racking up debts as much as $400 a week with creditors nipping at his heels. Adding to his mounting frustration, he had received no further payments from Pictorial Clubs outside of the $100 deposit they had paid him upfront. As a result, the *Laugh-O-grams* series fell far short of the proposed 12-film series, releasing only one updated fairy tale that December, *Cinderella*. During his latest financial crisis, that November, Walt's former partner Ub Iwerks quit the Film Ad Company to come and work for him. He primarily animated the title cards for Walt's early silent films before establishing himself as one of the century's premier animators and playing an important role in Walt's early success. But by then even his arrival could not save Walt's studio from pending doom. After the release of *Cinderella*, Walt could no longer pay his staff.

At the end of the year, to salvage his studio, Walt attracted an investor, a local Kansas City dentist, Dr. Thomas B. McCrum, who financed Walt to produce and direct a combination live-action and animated short for $500 under his *Laugh-O-grams* banner, *Tommy Tucker's Tooth*. For the film, Walt hired back some of his staff and auditioned students from Benton Grammar School for roles in the short, with 11-year-old Benton student Jack Records winning the part of Jimmie Jones.

By March of the following year, Walt tried to keep his dream alive by presenting his *Lafflets* series to Universal to distribute, but they passed. After this latest failure to resuscitate his career, he produced a single live-action, sing-a-long cartoon, a "Song-O-Reel," called *Martha*, featuring Iwerks in live-action, but again failed to entice a distributor.

Through the second half of 1922, Walt took out small loans— one for $2,500 and then another for $2,000 the following spring—to keep the studio afloat. During this ordeal, the one person he could always count on, though he was thousands of miles away, was Roy. Still hospitalized and recuperating from tuberculosis, Roy sent his younger brother "blank checks" to fill in the amounts of up to $30 to help him through his financial crisis.

BREAKING OUT ON TOP

By this point, Walt was desperate to make something happen. Inspired by Max Fleischer's tremendous success of combining humans in live-action with animated characters in his widely acclaimed *Out of the Ink-well* series, Walt decided he would do the opposite: "put the humans in with the cartoons." Thus, he created his first breakout series that would save his floundering studio, a new live-action/animated fairy tale series entitled the *Alice Comedies*, inspired by Lewis Carroll's *Alice's Adventures in Wonderland* and *Through the Looking Glass*, in which "a human character acted among animated ones." That April, after a talent search, he signed a heart-shaped faced, four-year-old "Mary Pickford look-alike" with long blonde ringlets, Virginia Davis, to play Alice in the first short, *Alice's Wonderland*. Walt had seen her on screen in a Warneker's Bread advertisement produced by Kansas City Film Ad Company. Instead of being paid upfront, Davis received five percent of the proceeds from the film.

Production of *Alice's Wonderland*, partially shot at Davis's Kansas City home with Walt directing, began that spring and lasted through the summer. The film opens with Alice (Davis) visiting the Laugh-O-gram Films studio where Walt himself shows her around and where she interacts with his first two major animated characters, Julius the Cat, a Felix the Cat knockoff, and Peg Leg Pete, a one-legged villain. After chasing and playing with them on the drawing board, she dreams that night while she is asleep of boarding a train for Cartoonland, where she cavorts with assorted cartoon animals.

That June, to pare expenses, Walt relocated to much more modest quarters in the McConahy Building that he rented, and barely finished making the film as he again ran out of funds. Roy, then recuperating at a veterans' hospital in Sawtelle, a suburb of west Los Angeles, wrote in a letter to Walt, "Kid, I think you should get out of there. I don't think you can do any more for it [saving his studio]."

A month before, Walt tried to secure a distributor by contacting several, including New York distributor Margaret J. Winkler, who expressed interest in seeing the film upon completion. After a series of delays, he finally completed the cartoon by mid-summer. By then, however, he could not afford to go to New York to screen the film for Winkler as more financial trouble ensued. Pictorial Clubs of Tennessee had filed for bankruptcy, thus unable to pay the $11,000 they owed him. Walt was desperate to pay off his creditors. By that summer, he owed $15,000 and things got so bad he started living at the studio. He was bathing weekly at Kansas City's brand-new Union Station train depot and eating "beans from a can and scraps of bread from a picnic." He considered giving it all up and heading to New York to work as an animator on the *Felix the Cat* cartoons.

Walt was much like his entrepreneur father in that when business bottomed out, he moved. Instead, he closed his "old rat trap" of a studio. In late July 1923, he sold his movie camera for first-class train fare. With only $40 to his name, Walt, wearing a checkered coat and threadbare pair of un-matching pants, boarded a train bound for Hollywood. Besides the lure of possible employment, he had two other strong reasons for going there: His uncle Robert Disney, who owned a successful real estate business, lived there, as did Roy, hospitalized for tuberculosis at the veterans' hospital in Sawtelle.

Walt arrived in the film capital of the world with only an imitation leather suitcase containing one shirt, two pairs of socks and undershorts, and some random drawings, and the coat and pair of trousers he was wearing that did not match. By that October, his Laugh-O-gram Films studio fell into bankruptcy. "Fed up" with cartoons and deeply discouraged at this point, he wanted to get out of the animation business. Not one to wallow in self-pity, however, he "learned a lot" from his recent setback and, as he put it, "turned my eyes to Hollywood, where I decided I would go and try to become a director."

Walt lived temporarily with his uncle, using his Hollywood residence at 4406 Kingswell Avenue as a base. He visited several studios, including Universal, seeking a director's job or "anything" to learn the business. He came close to landing an assistant director job at one studio, only for them to turn him down. With no offers, he wondered if he was "too late" to make a name for himself, but concluded: "When you can't get a job, you start your own business."

Walt returned to his first love—animation. Late that August, he informed Winkler that he had relocated to Hollywood and was going to set up a new studio at "one of the studios" in the area. If he was ever to reestablish himself, Winkler remained Walt's most viable option for distributing his films. She had distributed with great success Max Fleischer's *Out of the Inkwell* and Pat Sullivan's *Felix the Cat* cartoon series, but was on the verge of losing both and therefore wanted to secure distribution rights to Walt's *Alice* series.

Walt finally sent her a print of his unreleased *Alice*. By mid-October, she telegraphed him with an offer to distribute six *Alice* shorts and pay him $1,500 each, "immediately on delivery," with an option for 12 more films. Not included for distribution was his film *Alice's Wonderland*, as it was property of Laugh-O-gram Films and tied up in bankruptcy proceedings for Walt's former studio.

Again turning to his brother, Walt convinced Roy, a former banker who was better at handling finances, to leave the sanatorium after showing him Winkler's offer to help him seize this new opportunity. Leaving the hospital, Roy joined Walt to establish Disney Brothers Studio. He sought finances for their new venture, but most banks turned him down. Instead, Elias and Flora, still living in Portland, loaned them $2,500, and Roy pitched in $250 he had saved from his monthly pension. Walt then convinced his Uncle Robert to loan them $500 to launch their new studio. Renting space for $10 a month in the back of a real estate office a few blocks from their uncle's home, they officially opened the studio on October 16, 1923, one day after Winkler's offer.

In the beginning, Walt and Roy lived on Roy's veterans' pension, as Walt bought a secondhand camera for $200, built a stand from scrap, and started only with a small staff to handle the inking and painting of animation cels. As with *Alice's Wonderland*, the new eight- to 10-minute silent comedies, starring Walt's original Alice, Virginia Davis, who had moved to Hollywood with her family, employed the techniques of combining live-action of humans in the same scenes with animated creatures and backgrounds. Later three others succeeded her: Dawn O'Day,

Theatrical poster from Walt's first foray into live-action and animation, *Alice's Day At Sea* (1924), from his successful *Alice Comedies* series.

Margie Gay, and then Lois Hardwick. As Davis later explained in an interview, the films "always had a little story where I would get into the cartoon through a dream or I was hit on the head with a baseball and suddenly I'd find myself in a world of cartoon characters."

Walt produced and directed the first picture, *Alice's Day at Sea* (originally titled *Alice's Sea Story*), by Christmas of that year. The live-action scenes were done with no rehearsals and usually completed in a single take as Walt did not always have enough film to do retakes. The daily grind and stress of his newest venture at times became too much to bear. He was rail thin and a heavy smoker, camping himself at the studio, as the constant worry affected his appetite.

SUCCEEDING BEYOND HIS LIMITS

For the first time in months, however, things looked promising. Walt enjoyed the kind of liquidity that had been lacking after he had launched his Laugh-O-gram Films studio. By that February, he delivered additional films for release, including *Alice the Peacemaker*, *Alice Gets in Dutch*, and *Alice Hunting in Africa*. They were so successful that he was able to pay off his debts during the next three years and move to a larger location at a small store at 4649 Kingswell, which he rented for $35 a month. It had one room for his staff and him, a second room for photographing the animation, plus a garage he converted into an office for an additional $7 monthly. Etched in ink on the store's front window was the name of their new enterprise: "Disney Bros. Studios." That year, they produced 10 *Alice Comedies*; the first six animated by Walt himself, while Roy worked the camera filming the live-action sequences.

Even with Roy handling the finances, Walt's strong desire to do everything perfectly caused additional financial hardships as "he kept spending more in trying to achieve a better result" and with their margin of profits "narrowed . . . sometimes disappeared." Part of the problem was his limitations as an animator; others were far more accomplished than he was. In May 1924, he remedied the problem by encouraging his old friend Ub Iwerks to move to Los Angeles and join his staff at a salary of $40 a week.

The addition of Iwerks around the time *Alice the Peacemaker* was in production provided Walt with a capable draftsman, but more importantly, a brilliant animator whose skills far exceeded his own. After Iwerks came aboard, Walt relied less on live-action sequences; instead used them as beginning and ending wraparounds, with the comedies becoming predominantly animated. Furthermore, Iwerks made an immediate impact in improving the mechanics and quality of animation, creating more expressive characters and greater consistency in character movement, besides later nurturing Walt's young staff of animators.

In 1924, Walt's relationship with Winkler became more contentious after she married Charles Mintz, who took over her company and was far more devious in his business dealings. He sent only partial payments for the *Alice Comedies* Walt had supplied. That August, Walt pleaded in a letter, "We need more money. We have been spending as much as you have been paying us for [the films] in order to improve and make them as a good as possible, and now that we are receiving only $900.00, it puts us in a 'ell of a 'ole." Mintz claimed he had cash-flow problems but, by year's end, doubled the amount he paid Walt for the next 18 *Alice* shorts to $1,800 per picture. Walt's financial wrangles with Mintz were only the beginning of his troubles.

Around this time, Walt fell in love with a dark-haired and vivacious girl—and the first cel painter he had hired—named Lillian Marie Bounds. The Lewiston, Idaho, beauty, born into a pioneering family whose father was a blacksmith, was nearly three years older than Walt. He hired her "on the spot" as his new "ink and paint girl" at his garage studio for $15 a week after she applied for a job as an assistant.

On July 13, 1925, Walt, sporting a mustache since that spring, married Lillian at the Episcopal Church of the Nativity in her native hometown. Walt's parents were unable to attend as Lillian's uncle and then chief of the Lewiston Fire Department, in place of her deceased father, gave her away. Wearing a dress she made herself, she giggled nervously throughout the ceremony. Walt was the second to marry, following Roy who three months earlier wedded Edna Francis, to whom he had "more or less been engaged" from before entering the Navy, with Walt proudly serving as his best man.

A month before, Walt imported two more former Kansas City animators to add to his staff, now an even dozen: Rudolf Ising and Hugh Harman. By then, Walt was no longer animating the films, deferring those duties to his animation staff and putting Iwerks in charge of the art department. Instead he served as the main idea man behind the stories and gags, characterization, and film development, directing others to see his ideas through.

Unable to re-sign Virginia Davis, who pursued a dramatic career with little success, to return for a second slate of *Alice Comedies*, Walt replaced her in 1925 with another precocious young starlet, Dawn O'Day. Enjoying the kind of commercial success he had envisioned, that year he added additional animators and produced 15 more *Alice Comedies*, beginning with *Alice Cans the Cannibals*, five more than the previous year. His expansion of staff thus required a bigger working space. So, a month after his wedding, he plunked down $400 to buy a vacant lot at 2719 Hyperion Avenue in the Los Feliz district of East Hollywood to build his own studio. By mid-February of 1926, he and his staff all moved to the new Disney Studios in the middle of a rainstorm, changing the name that year to Walt Disney Productions.

In 1926, one of the benefits of their newfound success allowed Walt and Roy to build their first new homes—"kit" homes—for $16,000 on adjoining lots on Lyric Avenue in the Los Feliz district, not far from the studio. The houses were ready for occupancy by early 1927.

STEPPING UP AND CREATING FILMDOM'S FIRST STARRING RABBIT

While for Walt the *Alice Comedies* became a major stepping-stone, despite most films showing a profit, the series ended in the summer of 1927, after the release of the 56th cartoon, *Alice in the Big League*. Mintz was ready to move in a different direction. He was already engaged in discussions with Carl Laemmle, founder of Universal Pictures, about doing a new cartoon series. He wanted a cartoon series starring "a rabbit." In January 1927, Winkler, Mintz's wife, suggested having Walt develop such a series for them, with Mintz and Universal retaining all rights to any character.

Mintz approached Walt suggesting they retire the *Alice Comedies* series and develop a replacement. Walt complied, delivering rough sketches of rabbit characters and telling Mintz, "If these sketches are not what you want, let me know more about it and I will try again." The idea and final characterization, developed by Walt himself, was called Oswald the Lucky Rabbit.

In March, Universal approved Walt's sketches, paying him $2,250 per picture that first year to produce 26 *Oswald the Lucky Rabbit* silent cartoons (referenced in the opening credits as "A Winkler Production by WALT DISNEY"). To meet the demands of the new deal, Walt bulked up his animation staff, adding several more young cartoonists: Les Clark, Friz Freleng, Ben Clopton, Norm Blackburn, and Paul Smith. He left his animators in the lurch, however, giving them little warning about switching from producing *Alice* to suddenly doing *Oswald* until the deal was finalized. That April, he huddled with them to develop the story for the first cartoon, *Poor Papa*, made on a "rush schedule" that month.

Walt nearly fouled up everything with the first film. Universal and Mintz reviewed the print and Universal's response was "thunderingly negative." They refused to launch the series with the 100-foot film, deeming the animation "jerky in action" and "poor," and its story "merely a succession of unrelated gags." As for Oswald himself, they found him far from "funny" and too "elderly, sloppy, and fat," expecting him to be akin to popular movie comedians of that era—"neat and dapper chaps" and "young and romantic"—that the public would adore.

Disappointed, Walt went back to the drawing board and realized they were right. For his first all-cartoon venture to be successful, Oswald needed to be an attractive central character featured in stronger storylines. He revamped the character with Iwerks. The new Oswald that emerged was "a younger character, peppy, alert, saucy and venturesome."

Poor Papa was shelved, in the meantime. More than a year after Oswald became established, only then was it released. Instead, on July 4,

Poster art to the Oswald the Lucky Rabbit cartoon, *The Ol' Swimmin' Hole* (1928), the character that producer Charles Mintz took from Disney before his creation of Mickey Mouse.

1927, Oswald made his screen debut in the second cartoon Walt directed, *Trolley Troubles*. Frenetically paced, the one-reel silent cartoon, typical of most at that time, features Oswald as a Toonerville trolley car conductor coping through a succession of riotous encounters on the rails, held together by a string of slapstick gags, until his trolley finally plummets off a cliff into the watery depths below. Miraculously, the inventive and resilient rabbit resurfaces. Using the base of his trolley, he "rows off into the distance."

Trolley Troubles turned out to be exactly what Universal and Mintz had hoped for—a major hit that struck an immediate chord with movie audiences and critics alike. *Moving Picture World* praised Walt's rabbit as "bright, speedy and genuinely amusing," while *Motion Picture News* called the film "chock-full of humor." Despite the series' simplistic plots and slapstick humor, Walt's *Oswald the Lucky Rabbit* became his studio's first major cartoon star, one that grew in popularity and prompted offers to use the character in licensed merchandise. Walt directed eight more Oswald cartoons—a new cartoon every two weeks—starting with *Oh, Teacher!*

Whatever hopes Walt had of Oswald becoming a mainstay were dashed with a series events starting in 1927 that contributed to his downfall. Like his overdemanding father, Walt had become "an overbearing boss," alienating many of his animators who had become so disgusted they were ready to jump ship. Walt became intolerable as the pressures of operating the studio, now with a payroll of a dozen staff members and 26 new *Oswalds* on order, had taken a tremendous toll on the no-nonsense animator who desired perfection.

That summer, Mintz and his brother-in-law George Winkler were already working behind the scenes to take Oswald from Walt, recruiting several of his animators, including Iwerks, to animate the series without him. In early February 1928, the whole issue reached a crescendo when Walt traveled to New York with Lillian. He visited Mintz and Winkler at Mintz's office on 42nd Street to negotiate renewing his contract, but they rebuffed his original request for a raise—from $2,250 to $2,500 a picture, with Mintz countering with far less: $1,800 apiece. The figure would result in huge losses per picture for Walt's studio, something he could ill afford. Walt stalled on giving Mintz an immediate answer and went back to his hotel room. Discouraged, he wrote Roy and said, "I believe whatever does happen is for the best."

They met again later. Mintz countered with a second offer: paying Walt for the *costs* to produce each cartoon, liberal salaries for his employees, and an equal share of the profits. Mintz reminded him that Mintz and Universal controlled all rights to Oswald. After nearly relenting, Walt declined their offer. By mid-March, they broke off negotiations with him, with Mintz and Winkler producing the series for Universal with their own staff of animators.

Walt was surprisingly calm over losing Oswald to Mintz and Universal. Traveling by train back to Los Angeles with Lillian, they stopped over in Kansas City on the way. During the long ride home, Walt would decide on a new course of action and character, a new star for his cartoons, that would be his Oswald, and soon everybody would know his name.

3

A Perfect Fit: A Mouse Named Mickey

After losing the rights to *Oswald the Lucky Rabbit*, with the future of his company bleak and only a few thousands dollars to his and Roy's names, Walt had to create a new character fast to survive. On the train ride home with Lillian, he spoke of many different animal characters—kittens, cats, and others—he deemed as suitable replacements, but any good ideas they came up with, other animators had already successfully done.

During his life, Walt told various versions of how he originated a replacement for Oswald, as did Lillian, but the fact remains that he dreamed up the idea for a mouse character on the train bound for the West Coast. As Walt told an interviewer: "I was coming back after this meeting in New York, and Mrs. Disney was with me, and it was on the train—in those days, you know, it was three days over, three days from New York—and when I said, 'We've got to get a new character' . . . well, I'd fooled around a lot with little mice, and they were always cute characters, and they hadn't been overdone in the picture field— they'd been used, but never featured. So well, I decided it would be a mouse . . . I had 'Mortimer' first, and my wife shook her head, and then I tried 'Mickey' and she nodded the other way and that was it."

Many years later, Walt's daughter, Diane Disney Miller, in her book *The Story of Walt Disney*, remembered the conversation between her parents differently:

> "I think I've got something," Father told Lillian. "It's a mouse. I'll call him Mortimer. Mortimer Mouse. I like that. Don't you?"
>
> Mother thought it over and shook her head. "I like the mouse idea," she said, "but Mortimer sounds wrong. Too sissy."
>
> "What's wrong with it?" Father asked. "Mortimer Mouse. Mortimer Mouse. It swings, Lilly."
>
> She couldn't explain why "Mortimer" grated on her. It just did."

Walt later added that his idea for "a cartoon mouse" may have been influenced by having a pet mouse while growing up in Kansas City. "I had [a pet mouse] during my grade school days in Kansas City. He was a gentle little field mouse. I kept him in my pocket on a string leash. Whenever things seemed to get a bit dull between classes, I would let him rove about on his leash under the seats and get laughs from the other kids. . . .Perhaps it was the fond memory of him—and of others of his clan who used to pick up lunch crumbs in our first cartoon studio, the family garage, that came to mind when we needed so desperately to find a new character to survive."

With three *Oswald the Lucky Rabbit* cartoons left to deliver to Mintz and many of Walt's animators ready to defect to Universal that June, Walt, who clearly created the character's personality, enlisted Iwerks to design its physical appearance. During their drawing board discussions, they settled on a cheerful, energetic, and mischievous mouse and "shy litter feller" who physically resembled Walt's Oswald the Lucky Rabbit. They called him Mickey Mouse.

Iwerks' initial design of Mickey, modified over the years, was rather simple: black dots for eyes, a tiny muzzle and nose, unusually thin legs, and a short, curled tail. Mickey was also much thinner, and his movements were rather jerky like silent film comedy stars of that era. In contrast, Walt described him this way: "His head was a circle with an oblong circle for a snout. The ears were circles so they could be drawn the same no matter how he turned his head. His body was like a pear and he had a long tail. His legs were pipestems and we stuck them in big shoes to give him the look of a kid wearing his father's shoes. We didn't want him to have mouse hands, because he was supposed to be more human. So we gave him gloves. Five fingers looked like too much on such a little figure, so we took one away. That was just one less finger to animate."

Walt proceeded to produce two *Mickey Mouse* shorts to introduce his new star to filmgoers without securing a distributor first, to maintain more control over the property. He and Iwerks kept their new creation under wraps, as did Roy. Walt developed a storyline for the first *Mickey Mouse* cartoon he produced and codirected with Iwerks, based on the historic transatlantic flight of aviator Charles Lindbergh, titled *Plane Crazy*. Iwerks animated the entire cartoon behind a locked door in a period of about two weeks, amassing a phenomenal 700 drawings a day, an impressive rate for one animator and breaking the record previously held by animator Bill Nolan, who did 600 a day while working on George Herriman's *Krazy Kat*. Walt kept any evidence of the cartoon he and Iwerks were making from their fellow animators, even building "a makeshift workshop" in his Lyric Avenue home garage where Lilly, Roy's wife Edna, and Walt's sister-in-law, Hazel Sewell, inked and painted Iwerks's animated renderings.

On May 15, 1928, Walt previewed *Plane Crazy* at a movie house on Sunset Boulevard accompanied by music played by the theater organist. The response to the film was encouraging, and Walt and Roy produced a second picture with their own money, *Gallopin' Gaucho*, which Walt and Iwerks codirected. This time he did so sans the veil of secrecy as his defector animators had already joined Mintz's studio.

Walt sought a distributor for the series, screening *Plane Crazy* for MGM executives, who passed. Concluding he would have a much better chance of selling the series to a New York distributor, he contacted local film dealer E. J. Denison to help him find one. As part of any deal, Walt wanted $3,000 per cartoon in advance with a one- or two-year option to produce 26 *Mickey Mouse* cartoons annually. As hard as he tried, Denison could not find a buyer. They were reportedly "aghast" after the screenings. One said to Walt, "It's no use, Walt. Nobody's ever heard of Mickey Mouse."

WHISTLING TO A NEW TOON—ADDING SOUND

As Walt produced these shorts, something monumental was in the offing: sound in movies. On October 6, 1927, Warner Bros. released the first "all-talking" feature, *The Jazz Singer* (1927), starring Al Jolson. Despite its tinny and crackling sound quality, the movie was a huge sensation. Within a year, studios rushed to produce more films, capitalizing on this burgeoning new technology.

Recognizing the enormous potential of talking pictures, Walt decided there was no sense in making more silent cartoons and quickly produced a third black-and-white *Mickey Mouse* cartoon, *Steamboat Willie*, but with sound added. Released that May, this animated parody of comedian Buster Keaton's silent film comedy *Steamboat Bill Jr.* featured synchronized music, sound, and vocal effects. Earlier attempts were made to produce sound cartoons but the sound was not synchronized. In May 1924, Max Fleischer released the first sound cartoon, *Oh! Mabel*, using Lee De Forest's "sound-on-film" De Forest Phonofilm process. The film part of his popular *Song Car-Tunes*—or "Follow the Bouncing Ball"—series led audiences in theater sing-alongs of popular music on which the cartoons were based.

On September 4, 1928, 26-year-old Walt arrived in New York to synchronize the sound to *Steamboat Willie*. First, he visited different sound companies to see demonstrations of their patented sound technology, but "the variety of rates and the differences in technologies" only confused him. Following his impulses, he met with P. A. "Pat" Powers, a crusty old Irishman he immediately liked, who had his own sound-on-film system called Cinephone that imprinted optical sound impulses directly on the film. Walt waited to make his decision until after visiting RCA, where he was shown what would become the first synchronized sound cartoon that would be released two months before *Steamboat Willie*—Paul Terry's latest *Aesop's Film Fable, Dinner Time*— using RCA's Photophone Synchronization process.

Dinner Time was originally produced as a silent cartoon, but Terry added sound before its release, and synchronized the music, sound, and vocal effects. The film premiered on September 1 at New York's Strand Theatre, three days before Walt's arrival. For Walt, the cartoon was "a lot of racket and nothing else . . . and one of the rottenest *Fables* I believe I ever saw." The film is significant because, after RCA's screening, Walt noted in a letter to Roy that seeing it inspired him to create his first sound cartoon, with better sound.

That afternoon, Walt closed the deal with Powers with a $500 deposit to use his Cinephone process. Assisted by Iwerks, who again codirected with Walt, and animator Wilfred Jackson, Walt planned out the film and how many frames per second (every 12 frames) he needed to mark to synchronize the musical track to the action.

On the morning of September 15, Walt held his first recording session at the Strand Theatre where Terry's cartoon had debuted 14 days earlier, accompanied by conductor Carl Edourarde and his 15-piece orchestra to perform the music and two special-effects men to add sound effects. Walt, meanwhile, supplied the film's vocal effects—Mickey Mouse's distinctive squeaks, Minnie Mouse's shouts, and the voice of a screeching parrot ("Man overboard! Man overboard!"). In subsequent films, he provided Mickey's characteristic high-pitched voice as well and did not speak Mickey's first lines ("Hot dogs, Hot dogs!") until *The Karnival Kid* in 1929. The session went badly due to various mishaps, including Walt becoming so excited in delivering the parrot's line that he coughed it into the microphone. He left the session anxious and distraught, requiring a second session on September 30 to finish. With the process becoming so laborious, Walt became weary. In a letter, he wrote: "Personally I am sick of this picture 'Steamboat Willie.' Every time I see it the lousy print spoils everything. Maybe it will be a different looking picture with sound. I sure hope so."

One of Walt's biggest concerns was that audiences would "believe the character on the screen was making the noise," animator Wilfred Jackson, who joined Disney's staff that April, once said. ". . . It might just look like some kind of fake thing, and Walt wanted it to seem real, as if the noise was coming right from what the character was doing."

Of the synchronization process itself, Walt explained, "In the days of 'Steamboat Willie,' it was picture first. And then we used to put the sound on afterwards, and in those days you couldn't do what we call 'dubbing' today where you could mix a lot [of] tracks. It wasn't yet a science that you could get away with so we used to have to do everything at one time. And we used to have to run the cartoon. We'd have the fellows with the sound effects. We had the people with the voices. We had the orchestra going and everybody had to synchronize to keep that thing right on the button."

Upon completing the film, a reinvigorated Walt resumed his hunt for a distributor. In mid-October, Powers arranged for Walt to screen *Steamboat Willie* for Universal Pictures president Robert Cochran and several other executives. They liked the film and wanted to premiere it with the studio's new feature-length "talkie," *Melody of Love*, at New York's Colony Theatre on the condition that if audiences loved the cartoon, they would contract him to produce 26 more *Mickey Mouse* cartoons in 1928, and 52 more in 1929. Walt demurred. So long as Universal had Charles Mintz, his former distributor who stole *Oswald the Lucky Rabbit* from him, under contract, he could not accept. He made overtures to MGM, Paramount Pictures, and the Film Booking Office, but with no luck. Walt was in such dire financial straits after spending nearly two months in New York, costing him close to $6,000, that he met with Harry Reichenbach, an independent promoter-turned-manager of Colony Theatre, to screen the cartoon. Impressed, Reichenbach offered Walt $500 to run *Steamboat Willie* for two weeks. Walt countered with $1,000, and Reichenbach agreed, making the deal the highest ever paid for a cartoon on Broadway.

MAKING CARTOON HISTORY

As it turned out, Walt was on the right side of history. The experiment paid off exponentially. On November 18, 1928, promoted as "the FIRST animated cartoon and sound," *Steamboat Willie* opened, becoming the most successful synchronized sound cartoon in history. The short was shown every night for two consecutive weeks, with Walt attending every showing. The *New York Times* called the film ". . .an ingenious piece of work with a good deal of fun," while *Variety* raved that the union of sound and animation ". . . brought forth laughs galore."

Afterwards, Walt was inundated with offers from film distributors fielded by Powers, also acting as his sales agent. He insisted on a negative advance of $5,000 against a 60-40 split of profits after the distributor recouped the advance and expenses. Furthermore, he wanted to be paid by the week, remain independent, and retain full ownership of the cartoons. Unfortunately, Walt's talks followed the same pattern as before. Distributors were unwilling to accept any deal less than contracting him to animate the films or buy them outright. So they all turned him down.

With nowhere else to turn, a defeated Walt struck a deal with Powers to distribute *Steamboat Willie* and subsequent *Mickey Mouse* cartoons in exchange for 10 percent of the gross. Delighted, he returned home after three long, agonizing months with a deal finally in place. Going home to Lillian with a signed contract and money Powers had advanced him, Walt, unfortunately, had failed to read the fine print. His studio was obligated to pay Powers $26,000 a year for 10 years for using his Cinephone synchronized sound system. Learning the news, Roy exploded in anger, but with no other choice since they needed Powers and his equipment, he relented.

Shortly thereafter, Walt expanded his animation staff. He recruited two New York cartoonists, Ben Sharpsteen and Burt Gillett (spelled "Bert" in film credits), to join his Hyperion studio, along with Jack King and Norm Ferguson a few months later, to complement his dynamo head animator, Ub Iwerks. Then he hired Carl Stalling, a theater organist Walt knew from Kansas City, as musical director to score the music on his *Mickey Mouse* cartoons.

The sensational success of *Steamboat Willie* led to Walt producing a full slate of black-and-white sound cartoons. In early advertisements, credit was given as "A Walt Disney Comic, drawn by Ub Iwerks." That November, Walt subsequently added sound to *Plane Crazy, Gallopin' Gaucho,* and a fourth he completed, *The Barn Dance,* with Iwerks almost entirely animating the first cartoons himself, to release to theaters. In

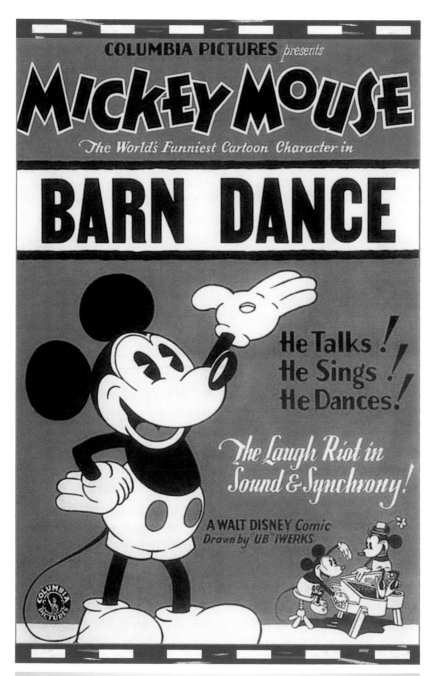

An original poster for the 1929 Mickey Mouse sound cartoon, *Barn Dance*.
© *Columbia Pictures*.

a short time, Mickey Mouse became widely loved. In March 1929, his amazing popularity was evident as Walt sat in attendance at the Strand Theatre for the opening of *The Barn Dance*. As he wrote Lillian: "Mickey Mouse is getting to be a very familiar character on Broadway—he is what is known as a 'HIT.'"

That year, buoyed by the public's response, Walt produced nine more *Mickey Mouse* cartoons, three of which he directed and six by Iwerks, whom he had elevated to director. Rocketing to national stardom, Mickey Mouse Clubs soon sprang up throughout the country.

At the outset, the *Mickey Mouse* cartoon series spawned the addition of other secondary characters opposite Mickey and Minnie central to its success, including Mickey's eternal nemesis, Pegleg Pete, who first appeared as a bear named Bootleg Pete in the *Alice Comedy*, *Alice Solves the Puzzle* (1925), and assorted animals such as Kat Nipp, Horace Horsecollar, and Clarabelle Cow. During Mickey's formative years, Walt drew liberally from many of his early silent *Alice Comedy* and *Oswald the Lucky Rabbit* cartoons, remaking and re-premising them as "talkies" with Mickey well into the 1930s. After *The Barnyard Battle*, Mickey and Minnie physically looked "more rat-like than mouse-like, less sympathetic" and, despite the novelty of sound, Mickey's acting ability was quite limited in these films. In time, Mickey's onscreen persona showed rapid improvement as did the stories in his cartoons—no longer simply "a collection of gags"—and as the country slid into the Great Depression, he became an "optimistic affirmation of their own values."

DREAMING BEYOND MICKEY

With success and money in his pocket, Walt never stopped dreaming. In January 1929, three months after the promising premiere of *Steamboat Willie*, he initiated another groundbreaking series, the brainchild of musical director Carl Stalling. Frustrated with tailoring his music to fit the action of the *Mickey Mouse* cartoons, Stalling suggested a New York recording session doing a "different kind of cartoon"—a "musical novelty"—where the action was subservient to the music, the opposite of the standard method used in scoring cartoons. He even proposed the subject for the first cartoon—a group of dancing skeletons, inspired by an image he remembered from an advertisement in the *American Boy* magazine—timed to his musical composition using parts of famed Norwegian composer/pianist Edvard Grieg's classical arrangement "March of the Dwarfs." Walt loved the idea. He had always wanted to do a series without continuing characters, akin to Paul Terry's *Aesop's Film Fables*. Thus, the *Silly Symphony* series was born.

After returning from *The Barn Dance* premiere, Walt found Iwerks had already developed the film's storyline, and by May 10, completed work on the animated graveyard frolic, *The Skeleton Dance*, animating every frame himself. The experimental film drew an unenthusiastic response from Powers after screening it for potential customers: "They don't want this. MORE MICE." Walt encountered a similar reaction at the film preview at a theater in Los Angeles. While audience members enjoyed the cartoon, the manager told him afterward, "Can't recommend it. Too gruesome."

Walt remained unconvinced. He did not see anything inherently wrong with the film. That June, he booked *The Skeleton Dance* at Los Angeles's prestigious Carthay Circle Theatre. Response this time from critics was glowing, with Walt subsequently sending copies of the reviews to Powers and the film playing at the Roxy Theatre and becoming a smash hit. Released nationally on August 22, *The Skeleton Dance*—with Iwerks's elaborate sequence of ghoulish spaghetti-jointed skeletons rising from the dead and doing a bone-clattering dance to the Stalling's lively prerecorded musical score—kept movie audiences riveted in their seats. The introductory *Silly Symphony* short further cemented Walt's place in the lexicon of sound cartoons. The film's rousing success led him to produce four more fanciful fables that year, directing three of them: *El Terrible Toreador*, *Springtime*, and *The Merry Dwarfs*.

In December 1929, however, the profitability of his studio came under question. Asked in an interview with the *New York Sunday News* if his studio was turning a profit, Walt shrugged and said, "Don't ask me if we're making money. I wouldn't know about that. I know we're getting by all right. My brother [Roy] turns up here each week with enough to pay everybody off. We haven't found time yet to sit around to count our profits."

Dapperly dressed Walt with wife Lillian and a stuffed toy version of his world-famous cartoon creation, Mickey Mouse, on the deck of the Italian ship, the *Rex*, crossing the Atlantic in 1930. © *Disney Enterprises. Courtesy: Walt Disney Family Foundation.*

The truth was Walt's studio could not turn a profit on making cartoons alone. By January 1930, the dozen *Mickey Mouse* and six *Silly Symphony* cartoons he had delivered cost an average of $5,500 per picture
to produce. After Powers took his 35 percent share of the profits as a
distributor, plus other costs he deducted, the margin of profit was razor
thin or not profitable at all. Walt was as much responsible as anyone
else for rising production costs. He insisted on producing "greater quality" cartoons, believing the studio's return on the films far outweighed
the added cost.

Roy was convinced that Powers was crooked. He enlisted attorney
Gunther Lessing to have Powers provide a full accounting of receipts
for their cartoons. When Walt was accompanied by his wife Lillian and
Lessing to New York to meet with Powers, he was unmoved by their
pleas. Instead he handed Walt a telegram bearing the news that he had
signed his head animator and long-time friend Ub Iwerks, paying him
$300 a week to create a new cartoon series that he would be distribut-
ing. Walt was shocked, especially since Roy and he had earlier made
Iwerks a 20-percent owner of the studio. Apparently, Iwerks's decision
was solely due to "artistic differences" that had developed between Walt
and him—and Roy knew of his intentions but had not told his brother.
Iwerks's decision had been building for some time. During Walt's ver-
bal clashes with Powers over finances, back at the studio, he turned
his anger on Iwerks, ripping his sketches off the drawing board and
throwing them across the room. Iwerks typically remained silent during
Walt's rages.

In the end, Walt lost two partners: Iwerks, who launched Iwerks
Studio to produce cartoons for Powers's Celebrity Pictures, and Powers,
who made a series of counter-offers that Walt rejected. In lock-step with
Iwerks's departure, Walt's musical director Carl Stalling joined Iwerks
after Powers doubled his salary to $300 per week. Despite Powers's
threats to sue if he signed elsewhere, Walt agreed to a deal with Columbia Pictures and studio president Harry Cohn to distribute the *Mickey
Mouse* series on the condition they also distributed his *Silly Symphony*
series, advancing him $7,000 per cartoon. Walt promptly paid off Pow-
ers in the amount of $100,000 (borrowing $50,000 from Columbia)

to regain control of the 21 *Mickey Mouse* cartoons he had distributed. On February 7, 1930, he effectively suspended production of his *Mickey Mouse* series to produce 10 more *Silly Symphonies* that year for Columbia.

To supplement the studio's revenue, Walt and Roy found the answer: merchandising Mickey. They licensed the first *Mickey Mouse* comic strip for newspaper syndication to King Features, initially written by Walt and drawn by Iwerks before his departure, after the powerhouse New York–based syndicate suggested doing a strip the previous June. First published on January 1930 in the *New York Mirror*, it went on to become a huge seller. Then, on February 3, 1930, Roy granted the George Borgfeldt & Company in New York the merchandising rights to manufacture the first licensed toys, figures, and other products bearing the design of the "comic Mice known as Minnie and Mickey Mouse."

With the release of nine new *Mickey Mouse* cartoons that year, starting with *Just Mickey*, Walt continued to tinker with the series, creating a new cast member who would become a major star in his own right: Mickey's faithful dog, Pluto, who first appeared unnamed in the 1930 black-and-white short *The Chain Gang*. Pluto's character evolved out of the natural brainstorming of making the film. As Walt told writer Tony Thomas, ". . .we were doing a short with Mickey Mouse. . .where he escaped from prison and they sent the hounds after him. And one of these hounds—we were foolin' around with this hound—it was on the trail of this runaway mouse, and out of that came this friendly hound character. And from there on we said, 'Well, we can use him.' And before we knew it, we had him as Mickey's pal."

In April 1930, after helming the 18th *Mickey Mouse* short, *The Cactus Kid*, Walt worked mostly as a producer while staying involved in story development. (In early 1931, Walt hired Fleischer Studios gag man Ted Sears and storyman Webb Smith, principally for story development.) He had established a strong core unit of animators—Norm Ferguson, David Hand, Les Clark, Ben Sharpsteen, Jack Cutting, Jack King, Dick Lundy, Tom Palmer, Johnny Cannon, Wilfred Jackson, and others—to maintain the increasingly higher standards of animation he set forth, while he served as an overseer of the productions.

Walt (center) confers with Bert Lewis, animator Burt Gillett, and story man Ted Sears at the Hyperion studio, circa 1930. *Courtesy: Academy of Motion Picture Arts and Sciences Library Collection.*

By 1931, Mickey Mouse had become a worldwide phenomenon, with the first-ever Mickey Mouse Club topping a million members as Walt upped his output of *Mickey Mouse* cartoons to a season high of 12, averaging more than 12,000 individual drawings to produce each short. Conscious of Mickey's worldwide success, Walt was cautious in how he handled his studio's top star. As he said, "I always thought of him [Mickey] as a personality. There were things he would do and there were things that he just couldn't do," he explained. "I would think of it this way, 'Now this is something that Mickey could do.' So we always thought of him as a personality . . . we kind of forgot the fact that he was a mouse."

When Walt first launched the *Mickey Mouse* series, he cast Mickey in situations that brought out the "little boy" in him. Later, he got away from that and characterized him simply as a mouse, but such changes were not well received. One distributor wrote him: "You've done something to Mickey, we've lost him." So he went back to his original casting of Mickey as "a little fellow . . . a mouse as small as you can get" opposite heavies like a big cat and comic situations that made him "cute" and "funny." As a result, Mickey held a special place in the hearts of audiences who viewed him as ". . . a nice fellow who never does any harm, who gets in scrapes through no fault of his own but always manages to come up grinning. . . ."

In late 1931, Walt was dealt an unexpected blow. He suffered ". . . a hell of a breakdown. I went all to pieces." He had pushed himself to the point of personal exhaustion on a number of fronts. He had expanded in 1930 the physical plant of their Hyperion studio, adding new offices, and he increased payroll the following year after adding more animators. As a result, he incurred more expense and debt trying to substantially upgrade the production quality of his cartoons, and he grew to expect more out of his animators. When they "let me down . . . I got worried," he later said, and he became more irritable. His new deal with Columbia put his studio in a severe "fiscal squeeze" after paying off Powers and falling deeper in debt. Pressure from mounting money worries caused Walt to snap at his staff for minor offenses. Sudden disappointments made him cry. He became so wracked with worry, he had many sleepless nights.

That October, after Walt finished his latest film, his doctor advised him to rest. He took a five- or six-week cross-country vacation with Lillian—their first nonbusiness trip since their honeymoon—to St. Louis, Washington, D.C., Key West, Havana, Cuba, the Panama Canal, and up the coast of Los Angeles—to recuperate and recover. He returned "a new man." Following his doctor's orders of varying his routine and exercising more, he visited the famed Hollywood Athletic Club two or three times weekly to swim, box, and do calisthenics, and he took up golfing and horseback riding. He routinely played nine holes in the morning in nearby Griffith Park before reporting to the studio, and left the studio early to go horseback riding with Lillian in the hills nestled behind their home. By December, despite an intestinal problem—some kind of "parasitic growth"—he developed that was treated, his health improved as he found work at the studio far "less nerve-wracking."

For Walt, as the coming months would show, he was far from finished making his mark on the world of animation.

Stretching the Imagination

Striving to perfect his animated film productions, Walt did something no one else had achieved: He made three-strip Technicolor cartoons. While he was not the first animator to use or add color, three-strip Technicolor far surpassed previous efforts in creating richer, fuller, and more vibrant hues.

By mid-1932, United Artists (UA) had become Walt's new distributor after he'd had a falling-out with Columbia Pictures. The new deal was a substantial upgrade over his former pact with Columbia, offering his studio $15,000 per cartoon, plus 40 percent of the film gross up to $60,000; an additional $1,000 at $60,000; and an added $2,500 at $75,000 as well. However, UA agreed to distribute the *Silly Symphonies* series so long as they were associated somehow with Mickey Mouse. To remedy that, title cards and posters promoting the series read: "Mickey Mouse Presents a Walt Disney *Silly Symphony*."

Walt had discussed with UA making one or more *Silly Symphonies* using the new process at an additional cost of $12,000 per short to produce. Seeing three-strip Technicolor as a way to boost bookings for his *Silly Symphonies*, whose popularity had lagged, Walt gambled. He persuaded Technicolor to grant him exclusive rights to the process through the end of 1935.

Afterwards by early June, Walt scrapped the latest *Silly Symphony* he had completed in black-and-white to redo it in full color. That film was *Flowers and Trees*. He had animators repaint backgrounds, and then reshoot the one-reel musical novelty, featuring the music of Mendelssohn and Schubert in color, a decision that ultimately had a profound effect on both the animation and movie industry.

Premiering on July 30, 1932 at Sid Grauman's Chinese Theatre opposite MGM's Clark Gable and Norman Shearer feature-length drama, *Strange Interlude*, *Flowers and Trees*—a blissful, moving story of a young tree who saves his lady love from a disastrous forest fire—created the sensation that Walt had hoped it would. While its plot was "pure melodrama" and its characters' "stock types," the film was the first to realize truly individual characterization along with simple, straightforward storytelling.

Becoming "the most imaginatively drawn cartoon from this era," his *Silly Symphony* series no longer was viewed as the poor stepchild to the studio's number-one property, Mickey Mouse, landing as many bookings with *Flowers and Trees* as "the hottest Mickey Mouse cartoon." The short was phenomenally successful, and within a year, the all-Technicolor *Silly Symphonies* became equal in popularity to Mickey Mouse—and later surpassing him—as Walt's studio's crown jewel. Even then, with the high cost, Walt shot two cartoons in the series that preceded and followed *Flowers and Trees*—*The Bears and the Bees* and *King Neptune*—in black-and-white, thereafter producing them entirely in color starting with *Babes in the Woods*, released that November.

Walt's success did not go unnoticed. For the first time that year, the Academy of Motion Picture Arts and Sciences recognized his remarkable achievements by nominating his studio and him for two Academy Awards in the "Best Short-Subject (Cartoon)" category for the *Mickey Mouse* cartoon *Mickey's Orphans* (1931), in which Mickey, Minnie, and Pluto cope with the sudden arrival of kittens left on their doorstep on Christmas Eve, and his stunning *Silly Symphony* cartoon *Flowers and Trees* (1932). On the evening of November 18, Walt accepted his first Oscar, awarded to him for *Flowers and Trees*, along with an honorary award for

Walt and his brother Roy, joined by Mickey Mouse, pose in 1932 with the special Oscar given to Walt for his creation of his famed cartoon rodent. *Courtesy: Academy of Motion Picture Arts and Sciences Library Collection.*

distinctive achievement for *Mickey's Orphans* and his creation of Mickey Mouse.

While admittedly a wretched draftsman, the 31-year-old animator's hands-on approach over all aspects of his studio's productions had much to do with the success of his cartoons. Maintaining ultimate authority on all facets, Walt often made rounds through the studio to review and discuss work with his animators and artists—the working men and women who made his studio's films a reality. He would show up in an artist's room, grab a piece a paper and pencil, and quickly illustrate an idea he had in mind, then stop in the director's room to discuss them, later laugh and joke with his associates as they worked out new stunts for a film, and drop into the writers' department and suggest a new twist to a story after looking over the shoulder of one of his writers at work.

Walt often found his drawing ability a source of discomfiture in public, especially when autograph hunters and dinner guests asked him to draw them a personal sketch of Mickey Mouse as a souvenir. In the late 1930s, during a trip to Europe, he took with him a sheaf of Mickey Mouse sketches drawn by one of his animators to give to acquaintances and at the same time cover his inability to draw.

According to his deep Midwestern roots and values, Walt gave credit to others for his success. As he stated in an interview, "We're an organization of young men. We have licked every mechanical difficulty which our medium presented. We don't have to answer to anyone. We don't have to make profits for stockholders. New York investors can't tell us what kind of picture they want us to make or hold back. I get the boys together and we decide what we want to do next."

One consistent theme throughout all of Walt's animated films that he produced then and beyond was his love of animals, birds, and nature, heavily influenced by his days growing up on a farm. "Those were the happiest days of my life," Walt once said. "And maybe that's why I go for country cartoons."

Walt only had one ironclad rule when it came to producing his films, no matter which ones they were. "Just one," he said. "Never do anything that someone else can do better. That's why we ordinarily side-step stories that could be done successfully in live action instead of animated action."

Walt certainly applied this rule, making his *Silly Symphonies* cartoons colorful and imaginative works of art based on classical works, fables, and fairy tales, and giving them stronger plots, unequaled in scope and beauty. They became his studio's first real attempt to animate lively and realistic human figures. As Walt's animators learned to work with color and experiment with plot, characterization, and photographic special effects, they achieved greater realism, character-ization, and personality, exemplified in this innovative film series. A direct result of that was Walt's efforts in 1931 to arrange for his anima-tors, who had problems "creating characters that were both convincing and entertaining," to take life drawing classes at night at Los Angeles's Chouinard Art Institute to improve their drawing abilities since very few of them had had artistic training. Shortly after that, animator Art Babbitt, who joined the studio in 1932, held weekly classes for his col-leagues at his Hollywood Hills home, using a live model to pose for them during their sessions. After three weeks, Walt offered to provide the supplies, working space, and models for the sessions before mov-ing classes to the studio.

Later, Walt established his own school at the studio, the Disney Art School, opening it on November 15, 1932, with classes conducted two nights a week by Chouinard teacher Don Graham, who was brutal in his assessment of the animators' weaknesses. Joined a few weeks later by Phil Dike and other top teachers who were added later, they trained studio animators in the importance of human anatomy, movement, musculature composition, quick sketch, animal drawing techniques, acting, and action analysis, bringing more realism and striking details to their work and becoming cornerstones of Disney animation.

That December 18, Walt became a father for the first time with the birth of his daughter, Diane Marie. Shortly before her birth, he wrote, "I've made a lot of vows that my kid won't be spoiled, but I doubt it—it may turn out to be the most spoiled brat in the country." Thereafter he showered her with toys and games and on Christmas of 1934 with a giant tree loaded with presents. He was careful, however, not to spoil her too much. As Diane later related, "Dad realized after a time that the more you want things, the better you like them." As she grew up and saw most of her father's films before they were released to theaters, he described her as his "severest critic." She would tell him if she liked the movies or not.

Eight months later, Walt and Lillian completed construction of their second new and much grander home, a 5,669-square-foot, split-level modern 12-room hilltop house at 4053 Woking Way in the Los

Feliz Hills, with panoramic views of the Pacific Ocean and Los Angeles below. Complete with an outdoor swimming pool, recreation building including a screening room, a bar, and a four-car garage, and Walt's personal favorite—a fully operational soda fountain—here they would raise Diane and eventually a second daughter.

GIVING CHARACTERS PERSONALITY

Walt's decision, meanwhile, to instruct his animators was one he would never regret, as evidenced in 1933's slate of *Silly Symphony* cartoons. Most notable was his third cartoon that year, *Three Little Pigs.* Based on the old children's fairy tale, Walt took six months to persuade his staff into making a movie version. During preproduction, his animators studied real-life pigs for inspiration and much of what they learned was carried out in their drawings down to the minutest detail. This included how healthy pigs' tails are more tightly coiled with no curl at all in weaker pigs. Earlier on, Walt and his crew considered putting the pigs on four feet, but instead reared them on their hind legs, giving the pigs more personality.

Released on May 27, 1933, *Three Little Pigs*, directed by Burt Gillett, became Walt's most famous and most successful *Silly Symphony* ever made, featured in movie theaters for several months. Unlike his Academy Award-winner *Flowers and Trees*, his animators realized extraordinary detail and more lifelike posturing and movement in their characterizations of the three little pigs—Fifer Pig, Fiddler Pig, and Practical Pig—and the evil Big Bad Wolf. Considerably more expensive to produce, the $60,000 three-strip Technicolor film—and its theme song, "Who's Afraid of the Big Bad Wolf?"—became a national hit with the Depression-era audiences, grossing $150,000 in its first 15 months and a profit of $88,000 in its first two years of release. The characters became so popular Walt starred them in a series of shorts, including *The Big Bad Wolf* (1934), *Three Little Wolves* (1936), and *The Practical Pig* (1939).

On March 16, 1934, *Three Little Pigs* trounced the competition, earning 80 percent of the votes by Academy members and Walt his second Academy Award. On the night of the awards, his head still bandaged from a polo injury, he received a rousing ovation from his

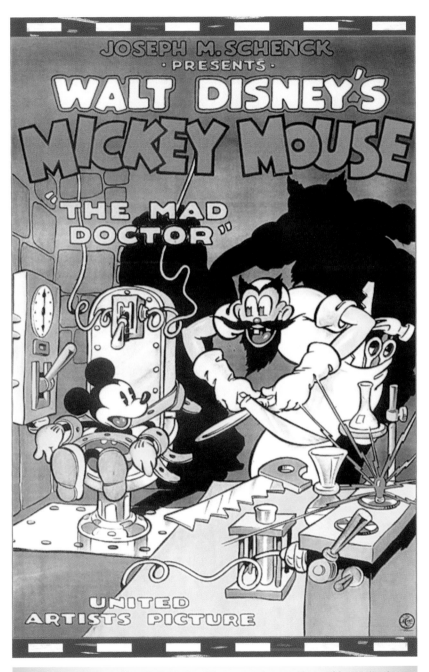

Poster advertising the 1933 Mickey Mouse cartoon released by United Artists, *The Mad Doctor*. © *United Artists*.

peers and during his acceptance speech referred to the thin-framed gold statuette as "Oscar," the first time the industry's pet name for the award was referenced in public. Iconic American humorist Will Rogers, serving as the ceremony's emcee, who played in the same polo match with Walt, joked: "Don't feel bad, I got whacked over the head with a mallet."

With his status rising as a filmmaker, Walt had taken up the sport of polo, first playing during his visits with Lillian to the desert resort of Palm Springs, California, and hiring a polo expert to train him. Palm Springs was one of their favorite retreats, and there they later built a vacation home in Smoke Tree Ranch in 1950. Back in Los Angeles, Walt persuaded animators Norm Ferguson, Les Clark, Dick Lundy, Jack Cutting, and others, and his brother Roy to join him in matches at Victor McLaglen's stadium on Riverside Drive. Later he played in competing matches at the lavish Riviera Country Club in Brentwood with Rogers and such luminaries as Darryl F. Zanuck, Spencer Tracy, and Robert Stack. Some years later after suffering a serious accident, crushing four of his cervical vertebrae, he finally gave up the sport, at Roy's urging.

The ensuing success of the *Silly Symphonies* cartoons left Walt cautious about how he made future installments. As he said, "We try to get something in the cartoon besides just nonsense. Some ideas such as in the 'Silly Symphony' where the idea of thousands of members of the animal kingdom preying on each other was carried out. We have to be careful not to get the sketches too silly."

With a superbly talented team of animators and supervising animators during the series run, including Burt Gillett, Wilfred Jackson, David Hand, Ben Sharpsteen, Graham Heid, Jack Cutting, Rudolf Ising, Hugh Harman, and Dick Rickard, the *Silly Symphony* cartoons would continue their dominance each year at the Academy Awards in the "Best Short-Subject (Cartoon)" category until ceasing production in 1939. Walt walked off with five additional Oscars for *Tortoise and the Hare* (1935), *Three Orphan Kittens* (1935), *The Country Cousin* (1936), *The Old Mill* (1937), and *The Ugly Duckling* (1939). Two others, also nominated, lost: *Who Killed Cock Robin?* (1935) and *Mother Goose Goes Hollywood* (1938).

On the evening that Walt accepted his fifth Oscar in a row, for *Three Orphan Kittens*, Academy toastmaster and comedian George Jessel asked recipients to keep their speeches short. After attempting to memorize his, Walt apologized, saying, "It didn't work." He instead read his acceptance from a prepared speech.

Of these films perhaps the most significant is *The Old Mill*, a standout film in many ways. Distributed by RKO Radio Pictures, which signed as Walt's studio's new distributor in March 1936, the Wilfred Jackson–directed short was the first to use a new technique Walt's technicians had spent years mastering—multiplane animation.

Work on the development of this revolutionary machine, which provided greater visual depth in animation by simultaneously shooting several layers of cels and backgrounds, was begun in early 1934 by members of Walt's staff, led by Bill Garity. This technical advance made possible for the first time in animated cartoons camera movements used for many years in live-action films that added a three-dimensional look, a greater illusion of more realistic and elaborate foregrounds and backgrounds to cartoons. Walt was not the first animator to experiment with improving the illusion of depth in animation, but he was the first to put it to good use and maximize its use in animated films.

In the multiplane animated *The Old Mill*, the end result was more realistic depictions in the characterization of the animal behavior, plus complex lighting and color effects, replications of rain, wind, lighting, ripples, splashes and reflections, three-dimensional rotation of objects, and timing used for dramatic effect. Walt and his animators put all of these techniques to increasingly greater use in additional cartoon shorts. And those techniques became the rich soil from which his studio's feature-length animations sprang, starting with *Snow White and the Seven Dwarfs* in 1937.

Walt's most embarrassing failure was the *Silly Symphony* film *The Golden Touch*, a retelling of the story from Greek mythology of the jolly King Midas whose granted wish of turning everything he touches into gold becomes a curse. In 1933, after director Burt Gillett joined Van Beuren Studio after making *Three Little Pigs*, Walt, who had not directed since 1930, became "so incensed" that he decided to helm the film himself. Using only two animators, Norm Ferguson and Fred Moore, he directed the film under a veil of secrecy. Completed a year later, he previewed the final cut at the Alexander Theatre in Glendale, California. Response to the film was overwhelmingly negative and viewed as "stiff and slowly paced," even by Walt himself. As word spread of his failure, Walt became so aggravated with a studio employee that he exploded, "Never, never mention that picture again!" and stormed off. Subsequently arriving in theaters on March 20, 1935, the film was quickly pulled from distribution. After the experience, Walt embraced his role as a producer and provided creative oversight, particularly over the area of story, on his productions, beginning with *Snow White and the Seven Dwarfs.*

ADDING A CARTOON QUACKSTER TO THE FAMILY

In the meantime, two years after making a splash with the industry's first three-strip Technicolor cartoon, Walt unveiled a new character that quickly succeeded Mickey Mouse in popularity: an irascible mallard, Donald Duck. On June 9, 1934, Donald made his first screen appearance as a long-necked, long-beaked, and bottom-heavy mallard wearing a blue sailor shirt and hat, as created by animator Dick Lundy in the *Silly Symphony* cartoon *The Wise Little Hen.*

Walt knew from the response from audiences and critics that he had something special in Donald. So, that August, he costarred him opposite Mickey Mouse in another *Mickey Mouse* cartoon, *Orphan's Benefit.* In the film, the gangly white duck is cast in a comic-relief role, making several frustrated attempts to recite "Mary Had a Little Lamb" and then "Little Boy Blue," as the audience of young mice mercilessly razz and torment him. As animator Ward Kimball, who helped animate the cartoon, remembered, "Well, the reaction that came pouring into the studio from the country was tremendous. The kids in the theater loved or hated or booed Donald Duck."

Animating Donald at first presented a huge challenge. Walt's animators had difficulty mastering how precisely a duck waddled on paper—confusing his walk between that of a duck and a goose. After further deliberation, they exaggerated Donald's walk instead. What made Donald memorable, besides his wild, exasperated onscreen antics, was his squeaky voice as provided by a good-humored actor, Clarence Nash, who began imitating animal sounds when he was 13. His favorite impression was doing a duck reciting the children's nursery rhyme "Mary Had a Little Lamb."

In late 1933, Walt was listening to voices he potentially could use in his cartoons when he happened to hear Nash on the radio. At the time, the Oklahoma native was working as a spokesman for the Adohr Milk Company, visiting schools in a horse-drawn milk wagon and making animal noises to entertain the school children. After hearing his hilarious recital of "Mary Had a Little Lamb" during an audition over the intercom in his office, Walt burst into the room and declared, "That's our talking duck!" and hired him on the spot. Initially, he had no idea how he would use Nash's talents but told him, "Well, I can pay you a little more than they're payin' if you want to come over here, and we'll find out what we can do with that voice."

Nash was on the payroll for a year before Walt brought him back. What kept throwing Walt all that time was the idea that the duck had to be a girl. Finally he said to himself, "Well, it don't have to be a girl—it could be a boy duck! So we ended up with Donald," he recalled. He cast Nash in the 1934 *Silly Symphony* directed by Wilfred Jackson, *The Wise Little Hen*, marking his debut as the voice of Donald Duck and Peter Pig. By 1938, Nash was earning a lucrative $200 a week at the studio, excellent money in those days.

By 1935, Donald's second year of existence, Walt produced the first *Mickey Mouse* cartoon in full color, *The Band Concert*, considered by many as the best *Mickey Mouse* cartoon ever made. In the one-reel cartoon, band conductor Mickey, during his playing of the *William Tell Overture*, is harassed by his malicious and mischievous and unruly costar Donald Duck, who steals the show by hawking ice cream to patrons during Mickey's Sunday afternoon concert. After famed conductor Arturo Toscanini first saw the new short-subject at a movie theater, he loved it so much that he bolted up to the projection booth and asked the projectionist to run it again.

After the birth of their daughter Diane, Walt and Lillian always wanted more children. After Lillian, nearing the age of 40, suffered another miscarriage in January 1937, they decided to adopt. They became parents for a second time to a two-week-old baby girl they named Sharon Mae. Neither daughter had the foggiest notion growing up of how famous their father was. "We weren't raised with the idea that this was a great man," Sharon later noted. "He was Daddy." While he and Lillian never produced a son as one of his heirs to his legacy, Walt always expressed great satisfaction over having two daughters.

By 1937, Walt was producing about 12 *Mickey Mouse* shorts a year, turning his high-pitch voiced rodent into a magician, a hunter, a clock cleaner, and a boat builder. The films, unlike previous installments, made more liberal use of slapstick and puns characterizing Mickey as "upstanding and moral" while his cantankerous costar Donald Duck always got into trouble. Bubbling under the surface, however, Walt had an intense desire to take animation to a new level and looming over the horizon was yet another series of important breakthroughs, ones that would ensconce him on top of the cartoon world.

Breaking
New Ground

Despite the continuing popularity of his cartoon shorts, Walt aimed higher. Applying the characteristic elements and techniques of his *Silly Symphonies* in much longer form, he broke new ground by producing the first full-length color animated feature.

Three years earlier, in June 1934, Walt announced production of his first feature, with an estimated cost of $250,000—five times his average *Silly Symphony*—a lushly animated adaptation of the Brothers Grimm German fairy tale, *Snow White and the Seven Dwarfs*. However, he was virtually alone in his belief that doing the movie was worth the financial risk, with Roy and Lillian objecting to the idea. After Lillian raised her objections, Walt pleaded, "But, honey, I've got our mortgage sunk into this movie. What have you got against the Snow White story?"

"I can't stand the sight of the dwarfs!" she said. "I predict nobody'll ever pay a dime to see a dwarf picture."

With his entire fortune wrapped up in *Snow White* and his bank "losing more sleep than I was," Walt forged ahead anyway. His long-term goal was to set up a studio organization so that every employee had ownership of the company. Revenue from *Snow White* would allow him to reorganize so it would "belong to the people in it."

But many remained skeptical and accomplishing such a feat proved far more difficult than Walt realized. Countless delays and cost overruns held up its production, costing him more than five times his original budget (subsequently dubbed, "Disney's Folly"): a whopping $1,488,422.74, an incredible sum for a feature film in those days, nearly bankrupting him a second time.

Walt's greatest challenge was crafting with his story men an acceptable story. As he said, "We've got to be sure of it before we start, because if it isn't good we will destroy it. If it is good, we shall make at least a million."

During story meetings in October 1934, Walt suggested giving the dwarfs (unnamed in the original fairy tale) names indicative of their personalities. From a pool of 50 suggestions, he settled on Doc, Grumpy, Bashful, Sleepy, Happy, Sneezy, and Dopey. However, he became wary of the comical approach in a subsequent story draft, afraid it undermined the story and development of the characters, including the Queen. Walt took over developing the story himself and fared no better.

Throughout 1935 as work on *Snow White* continued, Walt's usual boundless energy and razor-sharp concentration began to falter as he became increasingly nervous. Recognizing the same signs that caused his brother's previous breakdown, Roy recommended taking a 10th anniversary trip to Europe—to England, France, Switzerland, Italy, and Holland—with their wives. In a stopover in Paris, Walt was awarded the French Legion of Honor for "creating an art form in which good is spread throughout the world." Returning that autumn, Walt appeared much more rejuvenated and confident in *Snow White*.

By the spring of 1937, Walt employed the talents of virtually everyone in the studio every working day on *Snow White*, with the first cels inked and painted that January. At the same time, he continued producing new cartoon shorts to sustain his studio financially, while

(opposite page)
Original theater advertisement for Walt's first full-length feature, *Snow White and the Seven Dwarfs* (1937), produced in "marvelous Multiplane Technicolor." © *Walt Disney Productions*.

working to complete the feature film by its Christmas release. The end result was a superlative 83-minute fairy-tale spectacle, featuring an unprecedented two million hand-drawn, inked and painted drawings, never before seen by humankind. Even then, Walt had a hard time selling RKO Radio Pictures on the merits of distributing the film. One executive told him to downplay "the fairy-tale angle."

Asking why, the man said, "Because audiences don't buy fairy tales. We've got to sell it as a romance between the Prince and Snow White and play down the Dwarfs. We can call it simply 'Snow White.'"

Walt insisted otherwise, "No, it's 'Snow White and the Seven Dwarfs.' It's a fairy tale. That's what I put a million and a half into, and that's the way it's going to be sold."

DISPELLING HIS CRITICS

On December 21, 1937, *Snow White and the Seven Dwarfs* opened at Los Angeles's Carthay Circle Theatre with numerous noted Hollywood film luminaries on hand for its glittering premiere. The movie, with its combination of lifelike characterizations, homespun humor, heart-tugging drama, and snappy,

Walt and child star Shirley Temple show off Walt's special Oscars awarded to him at the 1938 Academy Awards for the first American feature-length cartoon he produced, *Snow White and the Seven Dwarfs*. *Courtesy: Cliff Wesslemann Collection, Academy of Motion Picture Arts and Sciences Library.*

memorable songs, including "Heigh Ho, Heigh Ho, It's Off to Work We Go" and "Whistle While You Work," delivered like Walt expected. Thousands of moviegoers flocked to see the world's first color cartoon feature. It became the number-one grossing film that year with a phenomenal $8 million in ticket sales—$4 million in the United States when average admission prices were 23 cents—putting Walt's studio for the very first time on firmer financial ground. The Hollywood community took notice of Walt's remarkable screen innovation, awarding him in 1938 a special Oscar, the second of his career, presented as a specially designed Oscar representing Snow White, flanked by seven little statuettes of the film's Seven Dwarfs in descending order.

As *Snow White* bolstered his studio's coffers, Mickey Mouse remained an iconic figure for Walt, though his popularity had begun to wane. In 1938, in answer to radio advertisers wanting for years to sponsor a show featuring his characters, Walt featured his most successful franchise character in his own weekly radio program on Sunday afternoons on NBC, *The Mickey Mouse Theater of the Air*, broadcast nationally from January to mid-May of that year. Sponsored by Pepsodent toothpaste, Mickey and company appeared in 20 exciting radio adventures traveling through time and space, thanks to the special powers of the Magic Mirror from *Snow White and the Seven Dwarfs*, with such storied characters from popular literature as Robin Hood, Cinderella, and Old MacDonald.

On the screen, Walt starred Mickey in his third Oscar-nominated short based upon the Grimm fairy tale *The Valiant Little Tailor*, retitled *The Brave Little Tailor*. Released that September, it became memorable for its beautiful production values and whimsical and inventive story, and as the second to last cartoon featuring animator Fred Moore's earlier original design and last appearance of the "pie-eyed" Mickey.

A year before ending the *Silly Symphonies* series, Walt introduced a suitable replacement, a series of cartoon specials, dubbed *Walt Disney Specials*. On November 25, the first short debuted, *Ferdinand the Bull*, based on the classic children's story. Continuing Walt's domination at the annual Academy Awards, it won an Oscar in 1939 for "Best Short-Subject (Cartoon)."

One day after its premiere, Walt's elation over his recent success was marked by sadness. On the night of November 26, nearly 11 months after his parents celebrated their golden wedding anniversary, Walt's mother, Flora, died of asphyxiation. Her death was due to a faulty furnace in a new home Walt and Roy had bought for their parents and which they had inhabited less than month. Needless to say, Walt and Roy were grief-stricken and devastated over the tragedy, something that haunted Walt for the rest of his life. Twenty years later, when a secretary brought up his mother's death in a casual conversation, Walt fired back, "I don't want that ever brought up in this office again," and then charged out of the room.

Emboldened by the success of *Snow White*, Walt increased his output of features by planning three more, all of which became crowning achievements in his career: *Pinocchio, Fantasia*, and *Bambi*.

Walt adapted *Pinocchio* from the classic 19th-century children's story by Carlo Collodi. Beginning filming in August 1939, Walt was determined to create "an even greater realistic movement" through the work of his animators. Besides continuing his practice of filming live-action versions of his features, begun with *Snow White*, for animators to reference and study the body movements of live actors, he also established a new department to build scale models of every character to help them make their animation more vivid and realistic.

Opening on February 9, 1940, at Hollywood's Pantages Theatre, *Pinocchio* stretched the technical boundaries of animation and give Walt's studio its signature song, "When You Wish Upon a Star." Sung by Jiminy Cricket (voiced by Cliff Edwards), it became a major hit. The film created a huge buzz of excitement. The following year, the film garnered two more Oscars for "Best Song" for "When You Wish Upon a Star" and "Best Musical Score," becoming the first time Walt's studio not only won in one category but both simultaneously.

Pinocchio did not fare so well, however. Hindered by delays in its release to Europe and Asia due to World War II, the movie, costing more than $2.2 million to make, took until 1947 to recoup only $1.4 million of its original cost and several rereleases to make a profit. The day after its release, Walt also informed his staff that the studio was again in a financial crisis.

After the success of *Snow White and the Seven Dwarfs*, Walt produced his second full-length feature about a wooden puppet come to life, *Pinocchio* (1940). *Courtesy: CineMasterpieces. © Walt Disney Productions.*

EMBARKING ON A NEW VISION—A CLASSICAL CARTOON MUSICAL

Work on *Fantasia* had begun while *Pinocchio* was still in production. Walt envisioned a film that visually interpreted classical musical arrangements as conducted and performed by Leopold Stokowski and his Philadelphia Orchestra. He believed that making the Technicolor musical was an important step, going beyond anything ever attempted in animated form. As he stated, "Well, 'Fantasia' was made at a time when we had that feeling that we had to open the doors here—this medium was something we felt a responsibility for, and we just felt we could go beyond the comic strip, that we could do something very exciting, entertaining and beautiful things with music and picture and color and things. . . ."

Fantasia was an outgrowth of a short-subject—and one of the movie's most popular sequences—that Walt had planned on producing in 1936 either as *Mickey Mouse* or the *Silly Symphony* cartoon *The Sorcerer's Apprentice*. By the late 1930s, he considered producing the short instead as a "comeback" film for his favorite rodent after story artists suggested Dopey from *Snow White* for the lead role. *The Sorcerer's Apprentice* became an animated version of German writer Johann Wolfgang von Goethe's poem *Der Zauberlehrling* (1797), and French composer Paul Dukas's concert musical piece *L'apprenti sorcier* (1897). Performed entirely in pantomime to Dukas's music, it featured a mystical Mickey Mouse as an unnamed apprentice (nicknamed by animators, "Yen Sid," Disney spelled backwards) whose misuse of the sorcerer's powers becomes disastrous.

Animator Fred Moore redesigned Mickey to make him more human and appealing. Previously Mickey was drawn as a series of circles of various sizes for his head, body, and ears, which limited his physical movement. Moore modernized Mickey by replacing his formerly black-dot eyes with smaller, rollable eyes with pupils, thicker legs, a shortened nose, a heavier, more flexible body with knees and elbows less angular, allowing for greater expression and giving him "an almost irresistible charm." (Moore's bold, "new" Mickey appeared a whole year before *Fantasia* in Walt's 1939 Oscar-nominated cartoon, *The Pointer*.)

Walt had planned to release *The Sorcerer's Apprentice* as a two-reel short-subject, but its high production values, lush color styling, and detailed character animation and effects were exceedingly expensive—$125,000—to produce. It was a price tag that he and Roy knew they would never recoup from a single release as their shorts typically cost an average of $40,000 to produce, which was $10,000 more than what cartoons produced by other studios cost. Instead, Walt decided to produce *The Sorcerer's Apprentice* as part of a full-length feature, originally titled *The Concert Feature* and renamed *Fantasia*. Beginning production in early 1939, he settled on eight segments: Bach's "Toccata and Fugue in D Minor," Pierné's "Cydalise and the Goat-Foot," Tchaikovsky's "The Nutcracker Suite," Mussorgsky's "Night on Bald Mountain," Schubert's "Ave Maria," Ponchielli's "Dance of the Hours," Debussy's "Clair de Lune," Stravinsky's "The Rite of Spring," and Dukas's aforementioned "The Sorcerer's Apprentice." He hired famed composer Deems Taylor to provide live-action narrative as a musical conductor in filmed wraparounds.

To make a greater splash, Walt wanted to premiere *Fantasia* on wider screens—double the normal size—and in three-dimensional sound in deluxe movie theaters on a reserved-seat basis. But with finances stretched to the limits, his bankers squashed such notions, with the film opening on conventional movie screens coinciding with the introduction of a new technical achievement he pioneered: stereophonic sound—or "Fantasound"—preceding stereo and surround sound by 20 years.

By the time *Fantasia* was completed, production costs soared to over $2.2 million (with music rights totaling $400,000 alone), becoming a costly amalgamation of live-action, animation, and music. While *Fantasia* marked the first film to feature the multi-channel stereo soundtrack known as "Fantasound," the film, released on November 13, 1940, in New York City, became well remembered as an ambitious marriage of animation, a "revolutionary integration of imaginative visuals" and classical music. One critic described moviegoers' reactions as ". . . shaken to their shoes and thrilled to the core by the teeth-gnashing, soul-storming cyclonic interpretations" of the music in the film.

Walt reviews color backgrounds to his all-musical, feature-length animated extravaganza, *Fantasia* (1940).

COMING UP SHORT

This time, however, Walt overreached. His extraordinary musical extravaganza, with its extremely large budget, was only shown in a dozen theaters in Fantasound as few theaters could afford his new technology, installed at a cost of $30,000 per unit. He also underestimated his audience. The public never accepted a popularized version of classical music. As a consequence, financially the film was a failure during its initial release. Not until the movie was rereleased in 1956, after previous re-releases in widescreen CinemaScope and in its original unedited form, would Walt's studio recoup its losses.

Although the public never fully embraced Walt's ambitious film effort, in 1941, members of the motion picture Academy recognized his unique contribution to the advancement of the use of sound in motion pictures, awarding him with an honorary Oscar, in addition to the Irving G. Thalberg Memorial Award, that same year. Film producer David O. Selznick, who presented the life-size bust of Irving Thalberg to Walt, heaped praised on Walt for his use of Bach, Beethoven, and Tchaikovsky, adding that the cartoon feature "contributed to the musical education of the public." Accepting the award, Walt, uncharacteristically, wept as he delivered his acceptance speech. "Thank you so much for this," he said sobbing. "Maybe I should have a medal for bravery. We all make mistakes. 'Fantasia' was one but it was an honest one. I shall now rededicate myself to my old ideals."

Unable to equal his original vision, Walt was always disappointed in the end result. For many years, he could not stand to watch *Fantasia* or *Snow White* for being "pressured into releasing both pictures for the Christmas trade before I was fully satisfied with them. I think Snow White's nose is too wiggly. And even though I have a tin ear musically, I recognize that some of the 'Fantasia' whimsy is overly cute."

Years after *Fantasia's* release, the film remained a sensitive subject for him. When a journalist mentioned how *Look* magazine called it a "flop" and another critic said it "was a qualified success," Walt fumed. "I don't pay attention to these so-called critics. The real critic is that great American public out there . . . if they like it I don't care what these so-called critics or reviewers say. . . ."

Walt insisted that *Fantasia* enabled audiences to become acquainted with classical music. That was its real contribution: "Young children, when they play records and see the music, they begin to appreciate" it.

Bambi, a book-to-screen version of Felix Salten's heartwarming 1935 story of a deer coming of age, *Bambi: A Life in the Woods*, was Walt's first all-animal feature and the last to be released. His greatest challenge was creating a convincing story with realistic animal characters that would entertain. For the film, he hired noted animal painter

Production cel from *The Sorcerer's Apprentice*, starring Mickey Mouse, as featured in *Fantasia. Courtesy: Christie's East. © Walt Disney Productions.*

Rico Lebrun to lecture his animators on structure and movement of animals, and dispatched his cameraman Maurice Day to photograph actual footage of forests, snowfall, rainstorms, spiderwebs, and seasonal changes of light as a source of reference. He also housed two live fauns—and eventually a menagerie of ducks, rabbits, owls, skunks, and other species—at the studio for them to photograph and sketch. With three features in production at once, including *Snow White* and *Fantasia* and his regular program of cartoon shorts, Walt employed a small unit of young animators—Frank Thomas, Milt Kahl, Eric Larson, and Ollie Johnston—to focus only on producing animation for *Bambi*.

Scaling back his other productions to make them more profitable, as production of *Bambi* slowly moved forward, Walt produced two more modestly budgeted features. The first was the story of a malicious dragon, *The Reluctant Dragon*, his first venture into live-action that cost $600,000 to produce. The movie bridges live-action of humorist Robert Benchley taking audiences on a tour of Disney studios and showing how cartoons are made with three cartoon shorts: *Baby Weems*, *How to Ride a Horse*, starring Goofy (with his celebrated "How to" series of cartoon spoofs debuting in this film), and *The Reluctant Dragon*, plus two other brief, animated segments, *Casey Jr.* and *Old MacDonald Duck*.

The second was a fully animated adaptation of a delightful book, *Dumbo*, by authors Helen Aberson and Harold Pearl about a big-eared baby elephant (real name, Jumbo Jr.) that learns to fly. Walt originally planned it as a 30-minute featurette, directed by Ben Sharpsteen, to be titled *Dumbo of the Circus*, but he expanded the film to a 64-minute feature. It was completed in a much shorter time span—a year and half—and at a much lower cost ($800,000) than his previous features. RKO, however, asked him to add another 10 minutes, to which Walt replied, "No, that's as far as I can stretch it. You can stretch a thing so far and then it won't hold. This picture is right as it is. And another ten minutes is liable to cost $500,000. I can't afford it."

To accommodate the overflow and need for a much larger plant, Walt and Roy bought a 50-acre lot in Burbank, California, in 1938, with their first $3 million profits from *Snow White* to build a brand new studio. On May 6, 1940, Walt Disney Productions relocated to its new facility that became the studio's permanent home. With its striking mulberry-and-green layout and air-conditioned buildings, it included an office suite for Walt complete with a stainless steel kitchen, a dressing room and shower, a piano, radio-phonograph, couches, coffee tables, and desk. Shepherding Walt's new studio through its expansion as they did for six years at the Hyperion studios was the same trio: Roy, George Morris, and Gunther Lessing. Walt earned the highest salary at $500 a week and Roy the second highest at $350 a week.

Walt leads a story conference with his crew during the making of *The Reluctant Dragon* (1941). *Courtesy: Academy of Motion Picture Arts and Sciences Library. © Walt Disney Productions.*

TROUBLING TIMES

Starting in September 1939, however, and during the uncertain times of World War II, revenues had begun to decline sharply. A month before opening their new studio, Roy advised Walt of the studio's troubling bottom line: a skyrocketing debt of $4.5 million—a culmination of profits gobbled up by the costs of *Pinocchio*, *Fantasia*, and *Bambi*, dissipating theater revenue overseas that accounted for 45 percent of the studio's income, and the cost of employing thousands of employees. As a result, in April 1941, his studio issued its first shares of common stock—600,000 shares at $5 a share. The sale raised much-needed capital of $3.5 million, temporarily assuaging its financial troubles, until a serious debacle nearly threatened the studio's future.

On May 29, 1941, Walt's 300 to 700 animators and their union, the Screen Cartoonists Guild, staged the first animator labor strike in history, with 1,000 picketers striking outside the studio within the first hour. The labor disagreement resulted from anger by animators over long-promised profit-sharing from *Snow White* and other contentious working conditions, which became a divisive wedge between the studio and them. Feeling betrayed three days after the strike had begun, Walt laid off his highest-paid animator, Art Babbitt, who headed the union's strike activities, and other union members. Making matters worse, he noted in a letter that the strike "cleaned house at our studio" and got rid of "the chip-on-the-shoulder boys and the world-owes-me-a-living lads."

In the midst of the strike, RKO released Walt's first of two completed features: *The Reluctant Dragon*. Premiering in mid-June, just weeks after the labor strike began, with the *Goofy* cartoon *How to Ride a Horse*, at Hollywood's Pantages Theatre, the movie was met by angry studio strikers picketing outside the theater and never quite recovered its cost. On July 28, after five long weeks, the strike ended after a federal mediator stepped in to arbitrate a labor settlement and required the studio to reinstate all striking workers, including Babbitt and others. In July, Roy announced plans for large layoffs that the union opposed, and then in August he shut down the studio for what was originally supposed to be two weeks.

That month, to ease tensions between his studio animators and him, Walt took with him and Lillian a handpicked team of animation experts—including director Norm Ferguson, animators Frank Thomas and Jack Cutting, story men Webb Smith, Bill Cottrell, and Ted Sears, and others—who he named "El Grupo" on a "goodwill tour" to South America as inspiration for new films. The trip resulted after the U.S. government originally asked Walt to embark on a hand-shaking tour to countries in that region.

Walt, Lillian, and his group of 17 and their wives toured the enchanted countries of Brazil, Argentina, and Chile. Returning to California that October, Walt and his animators produced four animated segments without any subsidy from the U.S. government. The first was a live-action/animated film costarring Donald Duck and little Brazilian parrot José Carioca to promote a "good neighbor" policy with Latin America, *Saludos Amigos*. One New York critic praised the 42-minute South American travelogue released in July 1943 as "at once a potent piece of propaganda and a brilliant job of picture-making." Donald and his chortling Latin-American amigo José Carioca were paired with a new character, a singing and "Iiieeee-ah-ah!" crying Mexican red rooster gaucho cowboy, Panchito, in a second feature, *The Three Caballeros* (1945), originally titled *Surprise Package*. Unlike the first, the latter lost money in the United States, and Walt subsequently cancelled plans to produce a third Latin America film, *Cuban Carnival*. Nonetheless, he was proud of the films, stating that "the government never lost a nickel on them— we paid for our own trip and the pictures, too."

While in South America, Walt received sorrowful news: His 82-year-old father, Elias, had died on September 13. After the death of his beloved wife Flora, Walt's father never fully recovered, and upon being notified, Walt told a friend on the trip, "I only wish that Roy and I could have had success sooner, so we could have done more for my mother and father."

Meanwhile, on September 15, the studio reopened once a settlement on laying off strikers and nonstrikers was reached, with Walt agreeing to all terms by the union and favored by the federal mediator, making his studio a "union shop" that paid union wages and benefits. The mood of the studio, however, was never the same afterwards. Only 694 employees returned to work, down from 1,200 before the strike.

A month later, Walt's studio regained some of its prestige with his next feature, *Dumbo*. On October 23, three days after returning from the Panama Canal, ending his 12-week South America tour, he attended the film's world premiere at the Broadway Theatre in New York. Loved by critics and audiences around the world, the story of "the little elephant that could" became an enduring classic, making $850,000 in profit. It

Walt tugged at audiences' heartstrings with his fourth cartoon feature, the story of a baby elephant with large ears that becomes a circus sensation, *Dumbo* (1941). *Courtesy: CineMasterpieces. © Walt Disney Productions.*

was Walt's last feature made during peace time with the Japanese attack of Pearl Harbor happening just over two months later.

Despite outward appearances, Walt was seemingly unpretentious, compared to other movers-and-shakers in the motion picture industry. He lived in a modest 12-room house in the Silver Lake district of Los Angeles, inhabited then mostly by Los Angeles businessmen. His marriage and home life was the least publicized compared to most Hollywood couples of that era. Away from the studio, his favorite pastime was "roughhousing" with his eight-year-old daughter Diane Marie and four-year-old adopted daughter Sharon Mae, acting out scenes from some of his future movies, like *Bambi*, and delighting in the reactions of his wife Lillian. On Sundays, Walt and Lillian held huge family get-togethers at their home that included Walt's uncle Robert, Roy, and his other brothers Raymond and Herbert, an insurance broker and mail-man, respectively.

Presenting himself as a modest fellow and a man of simplicity, Walt drove a blue coupe to the studio, but he also owned a much bigger car driven by his personal chauffeur. While many people viewed him as a celebrity, he never thought of himself this way. He once said that "being a celebrity has never helped me make a better picture or a good shot in a polo game or command the obedience of my daughter or impress my wife."

Nonetheless, Walt was sensitive to how others perceived him. After reading a magazine article that stated men who wore mustaches were conceited, he shaved his off, only to later grow it back. As his uncle Robert said at the time, "I give Walt credit for holding himself just like a real sensible fellow would. He hasn't swelled up a bit."

AIDING HIS COUNTRY

Following the horrific Japanese aircraft attack of Pearl Harbor on December 7, 1941, the U.S. Army used half of the Disney Studios, including a soundstage, for the repair of military vehicles and antiaircraft guns and to house troops as a primary defense state to guard the nearby Lockheed Aircraft plant against a possible air strike. Rallying to aid the war effort,

Walt produced a series of training and morale-boosting films with the U.S. government for the armed forces and more than 1,200 military insignia featuring Mickey, Donald, and many other characters for American and allied forces. After meeting with the Treasury Department and IRS, Walt created one of the films to encourage people to buy bonds and pay "taxes to bury the Axis." Completed by the end of February 1942, the result was a colorful eight-minute documentary cartoon, *New Spirit*, starring Donald Duck in a patriotic short that concludes with a mighty chorus of "God Bless America."

At first, the Secretary of the Treasury Henry Morgenthau resisted the idea of using Donald to represent taxpayers until Walt persuaded him. As he told him, "You wanted me to get this message over, so I've given you Donald. At our studio, that's like MGM giving you Clark Gable. The Duck is well known to the American public and they'll go to theaters to see him. I can promise that they won't walk out on him and I wouldn't promise that they won't take a walk on your Mr. Taxpayer." As it turned out, the flag-waving short, enjoying a record 11,500 advance bookings before its March 15 release, became the first animated film nominated for an Academy Award the following year for "Best Documentary."

Walt produced a wave of other patriotic shorts featuring well-known Disney characters for the U.S. government and its agencies, including *Food Will Win the War* (1942), *Out of the Frying Pan into the Firing Line* (1942), and *The Spirit of '43*, a second film starring Donald Duck. In addition, he made films promoting the purchase of Canada war bonds made for the National Film Board of Canada, such as *The Thrifty Pig* (1941), *7 Wise Dwarfs* (1941), *Donald's Decision* (1942), and *All Together Now* (1942). Under the auspices of the Office of the Coordinator of Inter-American Affairs, Walt also produced the classically animated wartime documentary *The Grain That Built a Hemisphere* (1942), nominated in 1943 for his second Academy Award for "Best Documentary," and the following year an unassociated subtle propaganda short, *Reason and Emotion* (1943), also nominated in 1944 for an Academy Award for "Best Short-Subject (Cartoon)."

In his mix of propaganda films, Walt produced a unique, mostly animated advocacy feature-length documentary, *Victory Through Air*

Power (1943), extolling the strategic value of aviation fire power to turn the tide against "the Axis in World War II." Released in July 1943 and screened for President Franklin D. Roosevelt and Winston Churchill, despite his sales force steadfastly avoiding selling the film as "propaganda," the movie lost $436,000. Such losses only padded Walt's studio's already burgeoning debt of $4 million, with his bank's board of directors growing more concerned over their revolving line of credit with such mounting losses.

In August 1942, pushed back by the strike, Walt finally released *Bambi*. Despite its exceptional beauty and achievement as "his most naturalistic animation film," the exquisitely rendered production, unfortunately, was not well received by audiences. With America at war and given the mood of the country desiring more spirited patriotic fare, the "quiet and gentle" 69-minute film became yet another in a string of disappointments, earning only $1.2 million in the United States and $2.1 million overseas.

Met by a much more receptive audience a year later was Walt's timely Donald Duck wartime send-up, the Academy Award-winning short *Der Fuehrer's Face* (1943), directed by Jack Kinney. Originally titled *Donald Duck in Nutziland*, the color short, features a famous rendition of the Spike Jones and His City Slickers song of the same name recorded a year earlier. It follows the nightmarish adventure of a "heiling Hitler" Donald as a munitions assembly-line worker for the Nazis, with the famous German leader getting his at the end. As always, Walt contributed to the story. As Kinney later remembered, "Walt liked to contribute in story meetings. He was a very good editor and could spot story weaknesses like no one else. Also, he had an advantage, in that we were usually too close to the stuff on the storyboards."

Walt's other prized cartoon series that he produced, *Pluto* and *Goofy*, each continued to attract industry honors and recognition as well. Pluto, now a close second in popularity to Donald Duck, earned three Oscar nominations—winning for 1941's *Lend a Paw*, while Goofy was nominated for his first Academy Award for *How to Play Football* (1944), part of his series of popular "how to" sports cartoons.

DIVERSIFYING HIS INTERESTS

Still badly in debt after the war ended, Walt wanted to do bold new projects, but Roy remained more cautious, more concerned about the bottom line. Walt wanted to diversify. As he later stated, "I knew that diversifying the business would be the salvation of it."

Walt compromised by intensifying his production of more low-cost features in a shorter time made up of animated episodes "linked together by a tenuous storyline," much like 1943's *Saludos Amigos*, as well as live-action/animated fare, and his ongoing program of cartoon shorts. In August 1946, Walt produced his second film representative of this trend, *Make Mine Music*. This post-war film—generally regarded as a "Poor Man's 'Fantasia'"—instead of being based on the classical music of Bach and Beethoven, features 10 cartoon shorts set to popular music of the era by Benny Goodman, Nelson Eddy, Dinah Shore, the Andrews Sisters, and others, invoking a rich flavor of American pop culture. Making a modest profit, Walt was displeased with one element: the "Peter and the Wolf" segment, believing his animators were "capable of much better."

That November, his second feature arrived in theaters, the live-action/animated *Song of the South*. Adapted from Joel Chandler Harris's book *Uncle Remus: His Songs and His Sayings*, it told the story of a young boy who meets a sage, black, storytelling slave living on a Southern plantation. Premiering in Atlanta, Georgia, the movie, described by animator writer Martin Goodman as "seamlessly fused [film]. . .technically ahead of its time," gave birth to the memorable song, "Zip-A-Dee-Doo-Dah," sung by Remus in the movie and awarded an Oscar in 1947 for "Best Song." Controversy reared its ugly head, however, as charges of racism were slung over Walt's depiction of the Uncle Remus character. Despite mixed reviews, *Song of the South* became his studio's first financial success in years, earning a profit of $500,000. (Burly, bearded-faced actor James Baskett, who starred as Uncle Remus, also won a special Oscar for his performance despite Academy board members originally opposing the idea because he played a slave, making him the first African-American male performer to receive an Oscar.)

This 1941 edition was part of a series of four-color comic books published by Dell Comics featuring Walt's famous cartoon rodent.

Both films provided welcome relief to Walt's studio debt, which shrunk to a new low of $3 million from $4.2 million. With animated films remaining his studio's lifeblood, in 1947, he produced a third package of well-done animated shorts with little in the way of plot linking them together. He combined two cartoon featurettes under the title *Fun and Fancy Free*. This included *Mickey and the Beanstalk*, the production that had been halted by the war but Walt later resumed. A clever retelling of the famed children's tale *Jack and the Beanstalk*, it starred Mickey Mouse, Donald Duck, and Goofy. The other featurette was *Bongo*, based on the story "Little Bear Bongo" by Sinclair Lewis. The two animated shorts were bridged together by live-action sequences starring Luana Patten and famed ventriloquist Edgar Bergen and his dummies, Charlie McCarthy and Mortimer Snerd.

By September 1947, Walt had produced 118 *Mickey Mouse* shorts as well as two features, *Fantasia* and *Fun and Fancy Free*, since the rodent's screen debut 19 years earlier. In 1946, he hired Jimmy MacDonald to take over as the voice of Mickey. In an interview, MacDonald admitted that his voice had changed after having his tonsils removed, becoming a little deeper, and that "Sometimes I'm sorry I started the voice. It takes a lot of time and I feel silly doing The Mouse in front of the sound crew."

A year later, Walt wrapped up production on two new features. Up first was the mostly live-action film distributed nationwide to movie theaters in January, *So Dear to My Heart*. With original work begun in 1946 under the title *How Dear to My Heart*, the movie, based on Sterling North's book *Midnight and Jeremiah*, unfortunately, did lackluster business. Following such a dismal failure was his fourth animated compilation, *The Adventures of Ichabod and Mr. Toad*. Released in October, the film, comprised of two 30-minute-long stories—*The Legend of Sleepy Hollow* and *The Madcap Adventures of Mr. Toad* (later released as separate theatrical shorts) produced disappointing results. Walt's fifth packaged animated film at the start of 1948 was equally unmemorable: *Melody Time*, a mostly forgettable array of literal cartoon interpretations of popular music and literature that became yet another stunning commercial flop.

Walt in a promotional photo for his Academy Award-winning *True-Life Adventure* live-action documentary, *In Beaver Valley* (1950). *Courtesy: Hollywood Citizen-News.* © *Walt Disney Productions.*

That year, Walt launched a new film series following his mandate, "Let's do anything to get some action," setting his studio on a new course that became extraordinarily profitable: the live-action documentary series *True-Life Adventures*. Enchanted by documentary footage of Alaskan seals shot by the husband-and-wife filmmakers Alfred and Emma Milotte, Walt saw unlimited possibilities, although some who saw the same footage with him said, mystified, "You never saw anything so dull in all of your life."

Working closely with a capable technical and writing crew, Walt added music, clever writing and jokes, and reedited the "miles of boring seals" into water-loving stars of his first *True-Life Adventure* released that year (despite his distributor RKO Radio Pictures initially balking at the idea), *Seal Island*. This extraordinary achievement was one of the film industry's earliest nature documentaries, and, more importantly, it won Walt his first of eight Academy Awards for "Best Short-Subject (Live-Action)" and "Best Documentary" out of the 13 *True-Life Adventures* he would produce between 1948 and 1960.

In 1949, Walt and Lillian built a new house on a five-acre lot in the luxurious Holmby Hills district near Beverly Hills that, unlike most elaborate Hollywood mansions, had some added features—a projection room and "a playroom with a soda fountain," Walt wrote, "where the girls can entertain their friends without disturbing the rest of the household." As in their old house, the soda fountain was one of Walt's favorites. His daughter Sharon later recalled, "He'd go out there and make these weird concoctions that nobody would eat, including himself."

In addition, the house typified Walt's love of trains. After a horseback riding injury prevented him from riding in further horseback competitions, he made trains his new passion and built intricately detailed tiny miniatures. As Diane once related, "He'd come up to the dinner table and bring this little piece of wood he had [been working on] and sit there all through dinner and be so proud of it." The property featured a half-mile circle of one-eighth-size train tracks on which Walt would ride his own scale-model steam-powered train engine he built, complete with a 120-foot long, S-shaped tunnel and trestles. Adults could ride Walt's railroad by sitting on the tops of the boxcars. As Diane once explained, "Walt was not so much interested in a new house as he was in the property, so that he could build his train on it."

With the dawn of a decade around the corner, Walt's greatest fantasies were about to come true.

6

Making Dreams Come True

Throughout his career, Walt was like one of "the world's greatest gamblers." He plunged millions into movie ventures, always with an eye to the future and rarely questioning the risks. The 1950s, a period of rising prosperity, a booming economy, and prevailing anti-Communist sentiment in America, marked a dramatic departure for him. He would do markedly fewer animated features in favor of modestly budgeted live-action films, expand to television, and fulfill a nearly two-decade-long dream of opening a place where every kid's dream could come true: Disneyland.

Ending an eight-year hiatus, Walt started the decade producing an all-new cartoon feature, *Cinderella*. The $2.9 million budgeted fantasy was something he originally wanted to produce 17 years earlier—first as a *Silly Symphony* in 1933, and then again in 1940 after reading the first script. Directed by Wilfred Jackson, the popular fairy tale, arrived in theaters on February 1, 1950. It had the right mix of Disney magic: a handsome, single prince who becomes smitten with a beautiful young lady enslaved by her two evil stepsisters and a happy ending with love triumphing over evil. In time, the film made a profit of $85 million, but the biggest seller became the film's soundtrack, including the hit song, "Bibbidi-Bobbidi-Boo." The song, performed by comedians Dean

Walt in a colorful pose shot for *Life* magazine with Mickey in the background. © *Time & Life Pictures*.

Martin and Jerry Lewis at the 1951 Academy Awards (with Martin singing the lyrics, Lewis adding the "Boo"), was nominated an Oscar for "Best Song," one of three nominations overall, including for "Best Sound" and "Best Original Music Score."

Once teasing with his animators, Walt told them, "Actors are great. You give 'em the lines, they rehearse a couple of times, and you've got it on film—it's finished. You guys take six months to draw a scene."

Long attracted to doing live-action films, despite his distributor RKO Radio Pictures discouraging him from making such a shift, Walt followed his convictions. That year, he produced his first all-live-action feature, *Treasure Island*, shot entirely in England beginning on July 4, 1949, while taking his family on an extended trip there. The swashbuckling adventure, adapted from Robert Louis Stevenson's classic novel, was both a critical and financial success, making a profit of $2.2 to $2.4 million on a box-office gross of $4 million. More importantly, Walt's first foray outside of animation spawned several mostly profitable live-action period dramas—selling them "as a Walt Disney picture" and also produced in England: *The Story of Robin Hood and His Merrie Men* (1952), *The Sword and the Rose* (1953), and *Rob Roy, the Highland Rogue* (1954).

One of Walt's most enterprising live-action action-adventure films—and first made in the United States—was the big-budget *20,000 Leagues Under the Sea* (1954). It was directed by Richard Fleischer, the son of legendary animator Max Fleischer, and filmed in CinemaScope. Filmed on location throughout the Caribbean and on a soundstage, the production required creating a new soundstage, Stage 3, on the studio back lot, with a huge 90-by-165-foot tank for underwater filming, expensive sets, including the submarine *Nautilus*, and special effects—among them a monstrous squid. The battle scene between the *Nautilus*'s crew and the hideous, tentacled giant squid took eight days to film, with a fussy Walt redoing the scene until he was satisfied, at an additional cost of $250,000.

Starring an A-list of Hollywood actors, including James Mason, Kirk Douglas, Paul Lukas, and Peter Lorre, Walt's ambitious screen version of Jules Verne's literary classic became the studio's first live-action blockbuster. *20,000 Leagues Under the Sea* generated positive reviews, and audiences flocked en masse to see the big-screen underwater adventure, many riveted by the giant squid battle as Walt had hoped. A one-hour documentary Walt produced simultaneously with the film's release

Walt displays his record-setting four Oscars—the most ever won by a single individual—at the 1954 Academy Awards. *AP Photo.*

on its making, *Operation Undersea*, won an Emmy for "Best Individual Program."

In 1953, after winning five more Academy Awards for his *True-Life Adventures* for "Best Short-Subject (Two-Reel)" for *Beaver Valley* (1950), *Nature's Half Acre* (1951), *Water Birds* (1952), *The Olympic Elk* (1952), and *Bear Country* (1953), Walt produced his first live-action nature feature, *The Living Desert*. He was inspired by the story of a 10-minute desert film made by University of California at Los Angeles doctoral student N. Paul Kenworthy and his colleague Robert H. Crandall, who spent months filming animal life in the desert. Walt felt it was worthy of being expanded into a full-fledged feature. As he told producer/animator Ben Sharpsteen, "This is where we can tell a real sustained story for the first time in nature pictures."

Walt proved right. Costing $300,000 to make, *The Living Desert* was tremendously successful after its release that November, becoming the studio's biggest profit-maker in its history, with $4 million in revenue. More importantly, with the film being honored with an Academy Award in 1954 for "Best Documentary Feature," Walt earned the distinction of becoming the person with the most Oscar wins (four) in a single year. At the 26th Academy Awards, he won three more Oscars: "Best Short-Subject (Cartoon)" for the *Walt Disney Special: Toot, Whistle, Plunk and Boom*, "Best Documentary Short-Subject" for *The Alaskan Eskimo*, and "Best Short-Subject (Two-Reel)" for *Bear Country*, both documentaries of his *True-Life Adventures* series. Actress Elizabeth Taylor, sporting a tomboy haircut, presented both documentary Oscars to Walt, who, with his total of four statuettes, told the audience, "Just gotta say one more word. It's wonderful, but I think it's my year to retire."

Following these triumphs, Walt and his team of documentary photographers captivated audiences with three more nature features, all filmed in Technicolor:

The Vanishing Prairie (1954), *The African Lion* (1955), winner of the Silver Bear award at the 6th Berlin International Film Festival, and *Secrets of Life* (1956), honored with the distinguished Golden Bear award at the 1957 Berlin International Film Festival. This led to Walt producing his first *True-Life Fantasy* film, *Perri* (1957), the pictorial record of a young female squirrel's progression through life.

TAKING HIS ACT TO TELEVISION

In 1950, with television becoming the rage, Walt was offered $1 million to buy the television rights to his 350 cartoons. He flatly rejected it, saying, "The television people want to buy my films, but I'm not selling. Why should I? They're still good for movies. And because they're timeless, they always will be."

Instead, Walt used this thriving medium to his advantage, launching his Disney-branded family entertainment into millions of homes each week by starting with the debut that year of the NBC Christmas Day special *One Hour in Wonderland*. He asked Bill Walsh, a former gag writer for the *Mickey Mouse* comic strip, to write and produce the program. As Walsh later recalled, "Walt called me [to his office] and said he had decided to go into television and I was the guy who was going to do it. I looked stunned and said, 'But I don't know anything about television.' Walt smiled back at me and said, 'That's okay. Nobody does!'"

Hosted by Walt and featuring Bobby Driscoll, Kathryn Beaumont (the voice of Alice), and Edgar Bergen and his dummy Charlie McCarthy, the black-and-white special was a crafty promotional film for his upcoming animated theatrical feature *Alice in Wonderland*. Previously he had had adapted author Lewis J. Carroll's novels *Alice's Adventures in Wonderland* (1865) and *Through the Looking-Glass* (1872) in other forms—first for his live-action animated *Alice Comedies* in the 1920s, and again for the 1936 *Mickey Mouse* cartoon, *Thru the Mirror*. Similarly, as early as 1933, he had pursued producing a live-action film, *Alice*, starring former silent screen star Mary Pickford, before settling on doing a feature-length cartoon. Walt's interest in the project waned, however, as adapting the story caused myriad headaches and problems. With some 80 characters and the need for a better-defined heroine, developing the film required scores of treatments by different writers, more than 40 songs, and five sequence directors to make it a reality.

After producing *Alice in Wonderland* (1951), Walt later realized the problem with the characterizations in the film was that Carroll's Alice "wasn't a sympathetic character. She was a prim, prissy girl who bumped into a lot of weird nonsense figures. We fell down in 'Alice' because we were trying to please Carroll's specialized egghead public as well as the mass public. Well, I learned you can't please both."

Walt sails away with Lillian and their daughters, Sharon (left) and Diane (right), on the S.S. *Lurine* in the 1950s from Los Angeles to Honolulu.

Walt's realization came too late. On July 26, 1951, after investing $3 million into the production, *Alice in Wonderland* premiered in London, England, Carroll's home country, at the Leicester Square Theatre.

Loved by British film critics, reviews in the United States were more brutal. *New York Times* critic Bosley Crowther opined that "watching this picture is something like nibbling those wafers that Alice eats." Consequently, the film, though nominated for a single Academy Award a year later for "Best Musical Score," lost $2 million domestically, as Disney biographer Bob Thomas writes, "erasing the glow of prosperity that 'Cinderella' had brought" to the studio.

Walt hoped to correct his oversight with his next animated feature, an adaptation of Sir James Barrie's 1904 stage play and book versions of a high-flying boy, *Peter Pan*. First acquiring the rights to the property back in 1935, he actually developed *Peter Pan* over the course of two decades (original models of Captain Hook appear in one background shot in the 1941 film *The Reluctant Dragon*). In fact, *Peter Pan* was originally intended to follow *Bambi*, but production was halted after the outbreak of World War II. Furthermore, Walt set aside the production at times over his difficulties of bringing "warmth to the characters." The prewar designs were radically different in the final film, commencing production in 1951 and finishing a year later. Every single one of Walt's famed "Nine Old Men," his inner-circle of animators—Les Clark, Marc Davis, Ollie Johnston, Milt Kahl, Ward Kimball, Eric Larson, John Lounsbery, Wolfgang Reitherman, and Frank Thomas—acted as supervising animators for the final time together on the project. It was also revered studio animator Fred Moore's last credited movie, as he died several years later, and the studio's last film released through RKO Radio Pictures after Walt formed his own distribution arm, Buena Vista Pictures.

This time around, his studio's lovingly yet laboriously rendered *Peter Pan* paid off handsomely. *Peter Pan* opened on February 5, 1953, to glowing reviews and a tidal wave of business. The $4 million budgeted, 76-minute film redeemed the "glow of prosperity" Walt had lost with *Alice in Wonderland*, and nothing made him happier.

Walt continued making occasional one-reel cartoon shorts, mostly to be booked with his new features. Even then, with costs rising to $100,000 to produce a seven-minute cartoon and diminishing profitability, he had become much more selective in his approach. As he told columnist Art Buchwald in 1961, "I saw the handwriting on the wall

In 1953, Walt produced his 14th classic animated feature, this time based on J. M. Barrie's play about a boy who could fly, *Peter Pan*. *Courtesy: Cinema Poster Archive.* © *Walt Disney Productions.*

about ten years ago. I'll make an occasional short now to go with one of my features, just to keep the theater owners from booking some horrible short subject with my own picture."

Throughout the 1950s, as Leonard Maltin writes in his book *The Disney Films*, the quality of cartoon shorts Walt produced "remained exceedingly high." His *Walt Disney Specials* series, along with winning an Oscar for director Ward Kimball's CinemaScope musical showpiece *Toot, Whistle, Plunk and Boom* (1953), reaped six more Oscar nominations for such masterfully made interpretations of classic children's literature as *Lambert the Sheepish Lion* (1952), *Ben and Me* (1953), *Pigs Is Pigs* (1954), *The Truth About Mother Goose* (1957), *Paul Bunyan* (1958), and *Noah's Ark* (1959).

In 1953, studios capitalized on the technology of 3-D, producing everything from feature films to live-action and animated shorts, requiring special glasses for audiences to watch in movie theaters, and Walt briefly jumped into the fray. He produced two theatrical cartoon shorts released in 3-D, *Melody (Adventures in Music)*, a *Walt Disney Special* billed in advertisements as "The Screen's First Animated Cartoon in 3-Dimension," when in fact it was actually his studio's first attempt and not the first 3-D cartoon, and *Working for Peanuts*, a Donald Duck cartoon costarring those screwy nut-loving chipmunks, Chip an' Dale.

In the coming year, Walt's family expanded by two new members. On May 9, 1954, his daughter Diane married Ron Miller, an outstanding University of Southern California football star then serving in the army and who later became a rising executive in the studio. Their marriage produced seven grandchildren in all, including Walt's first grandson, Christopher, born in December 1954, and "the apple of Walt's eye." As Walt joked, "He's the first man I ever had in the family. You know, I've been henpecked by my women folks all my life."

Walt's stunning success in the field of animated features continued unabated with a canine romance story and his studio's first cartoon feature not adapted from a published story or fairy tale, *Lady and the Tramp*. Development of the property had begun as early as 1937, with writers Joe Grant and Dick Huemer penning the first treatment six years later. Walt became attracted to a short story he had read by King Features editor Ward Greene, called *Happy Dan, the Whistling Dog*, about a free-spirited mutt, and told Greene, "Your dog and my dog have got to get together." In 1943, he had Greene expand his touching tale into a short book, titled *Happy Dan the Whistling Dog and Miss Patsy the Beautiful Spaniel*. Walt started developing a script, combining Grant's and Huemer's story with elements from Greene's published work, dropping

Promotional half sheet to Walt's first animated feature in widescreen CinemaScope, *Lady and the Tramp* (1955). *Courtesy: Cinema Poster Archive. © Walt Disney Productions.*

the project until 1952 when Roy encouraged him—instead of doing another cartoon anthology feature—to resume production so long as he kept productions costs down. Despite strong opposition from Greene and an RKO salesman, Walt was adamant on naming the film *Lady and the Tramp*. As he bristled, "That what's it about—a lady and a tramp."

On June 22, 1955, when the 76-minute animated feature opened in theaters, audiences were treated to the rags-to-riches story of a naïve and pampered cocker spaniel (Lady), who lives with a refined, upper-middle-class couple—Jim Dear and Darling (voiced by songstress Peggy Lee)—and a stray, street-smart mongrel (Tramp). Costing an estimated $4 million, the heartwarming, entertaining CinemaScope endeavor, though not received warmly by critics, became a substantial hit. The drama entertained while tugging at audiences' emotions with such scenes as the now-famous one of the raggedy Tramp drawn into kissing the cute cocker spaniel Lady while sharing a noodle from a plate of spaghetti and meatballs during the restaurant's owner's accordion serenade of "Bella Notte."

TURNING HIS DREAMS INTO REALITY

Yet it was television that would herald another hallmark moment in Walt's illustrious life and career: building his long-awaited amusement park, Disneyland.

As far back as 1937, when *Snow White and the Seven Dwarfs* premiered, Walt mentioned to a colleague his dream of building a park someday designed for kids. In interviews, he claimed his vision for such a place originated when his daughters were very young. Saturdays were always "Daddy's day," Walt's day with his daughters. "So we'd start out and try to go someplace, you know, different things, and I'd take them to the merry-go-round and I took them different places and as I'd sit while they rode the merry-go-round and did all these things—sit on a bench, you know, eating peanuts—I felt that there should be something built, some kind of an amusement enterprise where the parents and the children could have fun together. So that's how Disneyland started."

The seed Walt planted took years to develop and come to fruition. He started with "many ideas, threw them away, started all over again," and it eventually evolved into a more imaginative and elaborate finished product of a "magical park"—a real-life fantasy land for adults and kids. He originally intended to build the park on eight acres of land for the enjoyment of his employees and their families next to his Burbank studios, but World War II made him put such plans on hold. As his plans later took shape, he realized that the eight-acre parcel wasn't large enough. So he initially set his sights on a 100-acre site outside of Los Angeles, accessible by freeway, to accommodate his vision of a so-called "Magic Kingdom" complete with a scenic railway, fairy-tale castle, flying elephants, giant teacups, rivers, waterfalls, and mountains. (In 1952, Walt established his own corporation, Walt Disney, Incorporated—renamed WED Enterprises, using the initials of his name—to handle its building, as well as his other activities outside of the studio.)

One issue, however, stood in Walt's way: the soaring costs. His estimated budget at the time of $7 million rose to an eye-popping $11 million. In 1954, with the nation's economy in turmoil, he said, "I could never convince the financiers that Disneyland was feasible, because dreams offer too little collateral."

Walt made his park a reality by turning to television. That year, he contracted with ABC to produce a one-hour weekly television series, called *Disneyland*, in exchange for a $500,000 investment by the network to build his famed amusement park. After some 160 acres of citrus trees and 15 homes were cleared to make room, construction commenced that July. Twelve months later, on a hot July 17, 1955, Disneyland became a place of fun and fantasy for families and kids of all ages. During the park's first two years of operation, approximately 7.5 million people visited. One was Walt himself, who showed up in person at least twice a week to see that operations ran smoothly.

In October 1954, eight months before its opening, Walt's hour-long *Disneyland* television series was launched on ABC. (During its 12-year run with Walt hosting, the name would change to *Walt Disney Presents,* and the show even changed networks, to NBC, in 1961—retitled *Walt Disney's Wonderful World of Color.*) As he did in his first television appearance in 1950, Walt served as the host, playing himself, and presenting animated cartoons and other original and existing films and programs. The opening of Disneyland was broadcast on the program as a live television special, *Dateline: Disneyland,* featuring Walt and many well-known figures from the worlds of film and television, including Bob Cummings, Art Linkletter, and Ronald Reagan.

The *Disneyland* series spawned Walt's success in another form: original live-action adventures filmed on his studio's back lot for television.

Walt welcomes the first kid visitors to Disneyland on its opening in 1955.
Courtesy: Anaheim Bulletin. © *Walt Disney.*

The hit of the series' first season was the three-part, hour-long dramas he produced of the legendary American frontiersman *Davy Crockett*, starring Fess Parker in the title role. Broadcast in late 1954 and early 1955, the series cost $700,000 combined and created a national craze. The coonskin-capped folk hero, displaying old-fashioned grit and determination, produced a flurry in sales of licensed merchandise and a hit theme song, "The Ballad of Davy Crockett," not to mention two theatrical features reedited from television episodes, *Davy Crockett, King of the Wild Frontier* (1955) and *Davy Crocket and the River Pirates* (1956).

"Uncle" Walt, as they affectionately called him, on the set with the original cast of *The Mickey Mouse Club*, his studio's most successful daytime children's series, in 1955 for ABC. *Courtesy:* Anaheim Bulletin. © *Walt Disney Productions.*

Walt also produced a second season of two additional *Davy Crockett* adventures.

A month after the *Disneyland* television series' second season premiere and three months following the opening of Disneyland, Walt introduced a revolutionary new concept in children's programming, *The Mickey Mouse Club* ("M-I-C-K-E-Y M-O-U-S-E!"). The program was the first "expressly designed for children." As Walt explained to his staff during its development, "But we're not going to talk down to the kids. Let's aim for the twelve year old. The younger ones will watch, because they'll want to see what their older brothers and sisters are looking at.

And if the show is good enough, the teen-agers will be interested, and adults, too."

The Mickey Mouse Club became hugely successful, selling more than $15 million in sponsorships its first season. First televised on ABC on October 3, 1955, the half-hour black-and-white filmed anthology series was broadcast daily at 5:00 P.M. into virtually millions of homes across the country. Hosted by "Head Mouseketeer" singer-actor Jimmy Dodd and occasionally joined by "Big Mooseketeer" studio artist Roy Williams, the show turned its young, pubescent, and energetic mouse-eared cast of Mouseketeers into national teenage sensations. The original Mouseketeers were Annette Funicello (the most popular of all), Tommy Cole, Cheryl Holdridge (who joined in the second season), Darlene Gillespie, Bobby Burgess, Doreen Tracey, Cubby O'Brien, Karen Pendleton, Lonnie Burr, and Sharon Baird. Featuring fun and entertaining skits and dance routines, the series also offered recurring live-action serials based on children's books, such as *The Hardy Boys*, *Spin and Marty*, and *Corky and White Shadow*, as well as old, theatrically released Disney cartoons starring Mickey, Donald, Goofy, and others. It produced an explosion of hundreds of merchandise tie-ins, including plastic-eared Mouseketeer caps and coloring books, manufactured by 75 manufacturers.

By 1957, Walt's television productions grew with the introduction of a third series featuring the black-clad, masked outlaw and real-life Spanish nobleman Don Diego de la Vega, *Zorro*. The high action/adventure series, starring actor Guy Williams as the famous masked avenger in 76 original episodes, also aired as four hour-long versions on Walt's *Disneyland* anthology series. As a result of its success, production commenced of more family-friendly dramas, mostly Westerns, which Walt produced, including *The Littlest Outlaw* (1955), *The Great Locomotive Chase* (1956), *Westward Ho the Wagons!* (1956), *Old Yeller* (1957), *The Light in the Forest* (1958), the last four starring *Davy Crockett* star Fess Parker, and *Tonka* (1958), further demonstrating his ability to produce top-quality live-action films.

Walt was criticized for doing too many Westerns. When journalist Lee Edson noted during an interview that, "Some people are annoyed at you for that. They think the man who produced a classic like 'Fantasia' shouldn't succumb to the Western craze," Walt shrugged and said, "The sponsors insist I do them. Don't get me wrong. I like a good Western, but I agree there are far too many of them."

DOING HIS PART TO SUCCEED

Sporting a naturally receding hairline and neatly clipped mustache against his sun-toasted skin, Walt grew comfortable with his role as a fatherly figure to generations, thanks in part to the exposure of his appearances on the *Disneyland* television series. Spending few of his working hours in his office, he typically roamed about the studio, popping in and out of offices, talking to workers, asking questions, listening, and making suggestions down to the most technical detail, and with a childlike fascination, intent on understanding how everything worked. One day while visiting Disneyland, he stood for an entire hour, absorbed in studying every movement of a gigantic animated crocodile intended for the park's Jungle Ride as the beast crept forward and opened its gaping jaws.

Walt's utter devotion to his work, an unyielding trait of his, continued to dominate his time and life. In many respects, commitments and projects ruled each day, along with the daily pressure of operating a studio in the black with 1,200 employees under his thumb. Lillian understood her role and never interfered. As she once said, "If it ever comes to a showdown between his studio and his wife, Heaven help me!"

Away from the studio, Walt kept a small circle of friends, and outside of going to the theater on occasion with Lillian, he preferred to enjoy his evenings in the comfort of his home with his family. More limited in his recreation and hobbies, he still enjoyed working with his hands. On the property, Walt had a red barn built down a slope from his home. Complete with a workshop, the barn was "an exact duplicate of my dad's barn on the old farm at Marceline, Missouri; I remembered every detail of it." The workshop was fitted with small precision power tools and hundreds of hand tools that Walt used whenever he spent time in the barn after dinner in the evenings making miniature toy

Walt strikes a friendly father-figure pose in 1953 with the most famous characters he created, Mickey Mouse, Donald Duck, and Goofy, for *Life* magazine. *Photo by J. R. Eyerman. © Time & Life Pictures.*

trolleys, horses and wagons, or doll-sized furniture, all with the "unmistakable Walt quirkiness."

During the fiscal year 1958–59, Walt Disney Productions posted a record profit of $3.4 million. Outside of Walt's office was tangible

Walt takes a ride down Main Street with a costumed Mickey Mouse at his Disneyland theme park. *Courtesy:* Anaheim Bulletin. © *Walt Disney.*

evidence of his enormous success, a trophy case with a shimmering display of medals and plaques and record number of gold Oscar statuettes. By "doing a bit of everything," as he once said—full-length features, television series, and a veritable tidal wave of character merchandise, including comic books, clothes, and toys, and revenue from his Disneyland amusement park—his studio's ledger was in the black. In part, he felt he owed his success to the phenomenon of television and in particular to his so-called "Happiest Place on Earth," Disneyland.

"Disneyland was a natural," Walt once reflected. "It was so close to what we're doing in film. I thought of it a long time, but very few people believed in it at first. Now look at it . . . Disneyland was just a flat plain of orange groves. It cost us $4,500 an acre. The bank recently appraised it. Know for how much? $20,000 an acre. Imagine. $20,000 an acre."

For Walt, eventually his run of good fortune dried up. In 1959, after risking producing another well-known fable as a full-length cartoon feature despite mounting costs and years of production, he suffered perhaps his greatest critical and financial disappointment. His $6-million spectacle and most expensive animated film to date, *Sleeping Beauty*, an idea he began developing in earnest in 1953 but set aside when he became distracted by his *Disneyland* television series and live-action films, flopped. As Walt later admitted, "I sorta got trapped. I had passed the point of no return and I had to go forward with it."

A surprising development softened the blow that year: the sensational success of his studio's first live-action comedy, *The Shaggy Dog*. The property itself had been around the studio for years. Based on *Bambi* author Felix Salten's novel *The Hound of Florence*, Walt originally intended to produce it as his studio's first live-action film in 1941. Then, in 1957, producer Bill Walsh updated the property, changing it to a teenager transformed into a shaggy dog by a mystic ring, and proposed it to ABC as a television series that executives found "too far fetched." Walt decided after that, "All right, to hell with those guys. We'll make it as a feature."

Starring the always affable Fred MacMurray, whose acting career was in decline, and Disney teen star Tommy Kirk, the movie, directed by veteran film director Charles Barton in his studio debut, stunned even

Walt and his fellow colleagues. The modestly budgeted $1.2 million black-and-white comedy ran off to earn more than $9.5 million in the United States and Canada. Thereafter, having proved his studio could produce live-action comedies as well as cartoons, Walt plunged more heavily into producing family-oriented comedies and features with his stamp of approval. Not all of them were nearly as successful. Due to the failure of *Sleeping Beauty*, and other films between 1959 and 1960 that performed disappointingly, including *Darby O'Gill and the Little People; Third Man on the Mountain; Toby Tyler, or Ten Weeks With a Circus; Kidnapped;* and *Pollyanna,* starring the brilliant young actress Hayley Mills, the studio suffered a huge loss—its first in a decade—of $1.3 million.

Perhaps one of the only bright spots in an otherwise difficult year was news of a personal nature. On May 10, 1959, Walt's second daughter, Sharon, married Robert Brown, later awarding Walt and Lillian with three more grandchildren.

In the future, Walt would have many more reasons to smile. The disappointments of the past would fade as he basked in the glory of his return to the top.

7
Planning for Tomorrow

At age 61, his brown hair flecked with gray and his ruddy face showing signs of aging, Walt remained the eternal, small boy inside, full of wonderment and a dynamic, imaginative force. He continued to put in a 14-hour day, usually dressed in an open-neck sports shirt, sweater, and slacks, flitting among his four-room office, story conferences, projection rooms, and taking long, rambling tours of the studios. At the end of the day, he would retire to the comfort of his antique-filled Holmby Hills home with Lillian, taking work home with him—reading or editing movie scripts or watching movies—every night.

Still a ruthless molder of talent, Walt continued to push his staff and artists to the limit to meet his vision for whatever project he was undertaking, and his unpredictable moodiness often kept staffers on their toes. In the morning, they would look out the window as he entered the guard gate, and if he smiled at the guard who greeted him, usually that was a good barometer of his mood. Offering perhaps the best insight into his complex personality was Walt himself. On October 13, 1961, upon returning to his boyhood home in Marceline, Missouri, to dedicate a new school named in his honor, he revealed, "I'm not modest. I'm scared. I'm not funny. I hide behind the mouse, the

115

duck, and a lot of other things." He added, "All I try to do and hope for is to do as well in the future as I've done in the past."

Walt's approach—his total preoccupation with quality—showed where it counted in the company's ledger. By late April 1961, he and Roy paid off the studio's remaining debt. By 1962, Walt had produced 550 motion pictures, more than 600 television shows, and lent his name to 2,500 books, not to mention reaping millions in royalties from licensed merchandise of his world-famous cartoon creations. All this produced $4.4 million in profit on a gross income of $70.2 million for his studio. Early that decade, seven of the top 50 biggest moneymaking films, published in *Variety's* annual list of top moneymakers, were by his studio.

Walt viewed his success in simple terms. As he told writer Bill Davidson in a 1964 interview: "There's no magic to my formula. Maybe it's because I don't have to account to a lot of other guys, like bankers and boards of directors. Maybe it's because I just make what I like— good human stories where you can get with people and which prove that the better things of life can be as interesting as the sordid things. It's the old fairy-tale formula with the happy ending. People like to root for Cinderella and the Prince. If there is a secret to what I do—and where maybe my competitors make their mistake—I guess it's that I never make the pictures too childish, and so they do not become strictly children's films."

Walt's trend of producing profitable animated and live-action films spilled over to the next decade. He produced two big-budgeted films, the $4.5 million live-action *Swiss Family Robinson* (1960) and $3.6 million animated *One Hundred and One Dalmatians* (1961). He also produced the prudently budgeted *The Absent-Minded Professor* (1961), Fred MacMurray's second starring film, and *The Parent Trap* (1961), Hayley Mills's second feature. The four films recorded a total combined profit of $19 million. With Walt being just about the only producer at that time who was making money "on a regular basis," neither *The Absent-Minded Professor* nor *The Parent Trap* were deemed "Oscar material" at the Academy Awards in 1961, passed over for the likes of the World War II drama *The Guns of Navarone*, starring David Niven, Gregory Peck, and Anthony Quinn.

Of these, Walt's latest animated feature *One Hundred and One Dalmatians* outperformed *Sleeping Beauty* upon its release. The story was about a single man (Roger Radcliff) and single woman (Anita), both owners of Dalmatians (Pongo and Perdita), who meet and marry and whose two dogs produce a litter of spotted puppies wanted by the evil Cruella De Vil. The movie was three years in the making, required the work of 300 animators, and became the first feature to use the revolutionary Xerography process (copying drawings and eliminating the laborious task of drawing characters multiple times over). *Time* magazine applauded it as "the wittiest, most charming, least pretentious cartoon feature Walt Disney has ever made."

The so-called "Disney magic" did not always translate successfully at the box-office, however. Walt's other live-action features through 1963 produced mixed results, including *Babes in Toyland, Moon Pilot, Bon Voyage!, Big Red, Almost Angels, The Legend of Lobo, In Search of the Castaways, Son of Flubber* (the sequel to *The Absent-Minded Professor*), *Miracle of the White Stallions, Savage Sam, Summer Magic*, and *The Incredible Journey.*

Walt had a pent-up desire to expand beyond his usual scope of films that audiences eagerly stood by. After seeing the big-screen version of the Pulitzer Prize winning novel *To Kill a Mockingbird* (1962), he told his son-in-law and then studio producer Ron Miller that he wanted to "make a picture like it." But he knew his audience would never accept such a film by him. "He was very frustrated," Miller later recalled. "Walt had created this image and he got locked in."

1963 welcomed Walt's first full-length feature in two years, *The Sword in the Stone*, based on a volume of T. H. White's original story of a scrawny young lad who becomes the legendary hero King Arthur. Walt became sold on the project after enjoying the 1960 Broadway production of *Camelot*. Not everyone agreed with him. None of his animators wanted to make the medieval film, including several of his famous "Old Nine Men," who were passionately more interested in reviving a project that lay dormant, *Chanticleer the Rooster*. Upon its completion, Walt criticized the work of his animators as "weak" and advised them to do better with his next animated film on the drawing boards, *The Jungle Book.*

Directed by Wolfgang "Woolie" Reitherman, despite Walt's criticisms, *The Sword in the Stone* garnered mostly favorable reviews and endeared itself with audiences. Debuting on Christmas Day, the 76-minute fantasy film, though not usually considered among the studio's true classics, became a financial success, earning $4.5 million and becoming the studio's sixth highest grossing movie of that year.

Walt's resolutely wholesome films, however, incited other criticism regarding whether he was squeamish about the word "s-e-x" and was a prude. He responded outright, saying, "Certainly I believe sex—the love a boy has for a girl—is natural. But I believe there are other kinds of love as well. There's the love another has for a child, as in 'Bambi,' or a child for a dog, as in 'Old Yeller.' What I look for are stories with a universal appeal. An American stand-up comedian is apt to flop in Japan, say, because his jokes are too localized. But my 'Parent Trap' was a smashing success in Japan, because the whole world understands the humor that arises from family life."

In the live-action movie *Bon Voyage!* (1962), Walt allowed a scene to be filmed with its costar Fred MacMurray being propositioned by a lovely Parisian girl near a sidewalk café, something he later regretted. "I caught hell for it," he said. "Never again."

When asked by one journalist, "What is a Disney picture?" Walt said, "Hell, I'm Disney, and I don't know. I've produced every type of picture except sick ones. The truth of the matter is I try to make movies to please my own family. We don't aim at children specifically. When does any person stop being a child?"

BUILDING TOWARD THE FUTURE

In the meantime, the always enterprising animator unveiled plans for a new university for up-and-coming artists and animators: "A completely new approach to training in the arts is needed. That's the principal thing I hope to leave when I move on to greener pastures. If I can help provide a place to develop the talent of the future, I think I will have accomplished something." In 1961, his vision culminated into a permanent trade school, California Institute of the Arts, or CalArts, an amalgamation of the Chouinard Art Institute and the Los Angeles Conservatory of Music, to educate students in all disciplines of the arts—dance, music, drama, visual arts, and film.

Breakthroughs in technology once again became a pivotal part of Walt's success.

By 1963, he introduced the latest technological advancement created by employee Lee Adams of his WED Enterprises (later renamed Walt Disney Imagineering): Audio-Animatronics. This process enabled once immobile characters to robotically move and talk and could be used in bringing to life human-like figures in future Disneyland attractions. That year, Walt unveiled his first use of this technology, with a mechanical toy bird he got in New Orleans, at his newest Disneyland attraction, the Enchanted Tiki Room. The bird was later followed by a "dancing man" Walt created by hand.

Despite such a busy schedule, Walt visited the park on average once a month. He had great interest in planning and improving the facility, with the same glow of boyish excitement, but due to his fame and notoriety, often walked fast through the park to go unnoticed by park patrons. "It's pretty hard to get around Disneyland when people are there. I mean, they're friendly, they're wonderful, and I love to meet them, but I can't stand still long because I'll—oh, I don't mind giving autographs. I think it's wonderful that they do want your autograph. But when I'm at Disneyland, if I stop to sign one autograph, before I can get that signed, there are some more up there, and it accumulates quite a crowd, and it always makes it awful hard to get away."

In 1964, Walt showed no signs of slowing down. On April 22, he unveiled his company's earlier innovation, Audio-Animatronics, in four exhibits—"dimensional type shows"—at the New York World's Fair. A major hit was an exhibit produced for the State of Illinois, *Great Moments with Mr. Lincoln*, featuring the first fully functioning Audio-Animatronics talking and moving Abraham Lincoln shipped from California to New York and later added as a Main Street attraction at Disneyland. Other WED company-constructed exhibits included the Magic Skyway and Progressland pavilions for Ford and General Electric, and *It's a Small World*, sponsored by Pepsi-Cola and UNICEF, equally popular

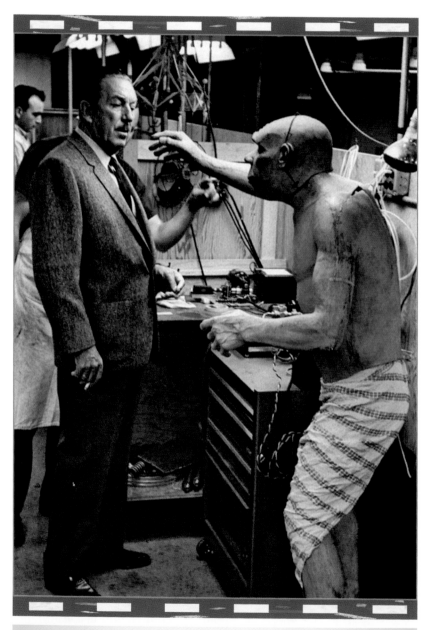

During a visit to the Imagineering division, Walt inspects an unfinished Audio-Animatronic pirate for Disneyland's *Pirates of the Caribbean* ride. *Courtesy:* Los Angeles Times *Photographic Archive, UCLA Library.* © Los Angeles Times.

with fairgoers. Walt also had on the drawing board plans for a ski resort called Mineral King, to be built near the Sequoia National Park, and another was a tourist attraction, Walt Disney's Boyhood Home, in Marceline after buying properties there as part of its eventual development. Neither project came into being.

That same year, Walt produced a potpourri of family film fare, some of them standouts, including *The Misadventures of Merlin Jones*, co-starring Tommy Kirk and former Mouseketeer Annette Funicello, *A Tiger Walks*, *The Three Lives of Thomasina*, *The Moon-Spinners*, and *Emil and the Detectives*. His greatest cinematic triumph, capping his extraordinary career as a producer that year, was the live-action/animated feature *Mary Poppins*.

For 20 years, after first reading author P. L. Travers's book about an English nanny who could fly, *Mary Poppins* was a property near and dear to Walt's heart. He first wanted to acquire the rights to turn it into a movie back in 1944. It took 16 years until Travers agreed to the deal, with Walt picking Robert Stevenson of *Old Yeller* and *The Absent-Minded Professor* fame to direct, and Bill Walsh to coproduce and cowrite the script. Walt played an important role throughout, editing, changing dialogue, adding visual flourishes, and interjecting other creative ideas into the various drafts of the script to his liking.

One of his studio's costliest films ($5.175 million) to date, the live-action and animated film costarring Julie Andrews and Dick Van Dyke (then popular on television's *The Dick Van Dyke Show*) did gonzo business. Opening on August 27, 1964, at Hollywood's Grauman's Chinese Theatre, the movie, which attracted widespread praise and cheers, grossed an astonishing $50 million worldwide and rose to the top of the year's moneymakers. "One of the most magnificent pieces of entertainment ever to come to Hollywood," wrote critic Hollis Alpert. One of the most memorable scenes remains Van Dyke dancing seamlessly in a blend of live-action and animation with four cartooned penguins.

Becoming Walt's greatest success since *Snow White*, *Mary Poppins* was also his first feature to employ the use of a sodium-loss process to make special-effects mattes on film. The movie was crowned with a record 13 Oscar nominations—the first time any of Walt's films had

Walt receives the distinguished Medal of Freedom from President Lyndon Johnson in 1964. *AP Photo.*

contended in every category. At the 1964 Academy Awards, the movie won for "Best Actress," "Best Song" (for "Chim Chim Cher-ee"), "Best Original Music Score," "Best Film Editing," "Best Special Effects," and "Best Color Traveling Matte Composite Cinematography." Presented with her Oscar by actor Sidney Poitier, British actress Julie Andrews, in her acceptance speech, said, "I know where to start—Mr. Walt Disney gets the biggest thank you."

Meanwhile, Walt was showered with an important honor himself. On September 10, 1964, President Lyndon Johnson bestowed upon him the nation's highest civil honor in the East Wing of the White House: the Presidential Medal of Freedom. The citation read: "Artist and impresario, in the course of entertaining an age, Walt Disney has created an American folklore." As flashbulbs from a cadre of newspaper photographers exploded around him, Walt smiled proudly as the President draped the medal around his neck. He never dreamed such a moment would come.

EXPANDING HIS ENTERPRISE

Over the years, Walt was often asked if there would ever be another Disneyland. He responded, "I think there will only be one Disneyland as such. Now, that doesn't mean that in some areas we might not develop certain projects that would be compatible to that area, that might very well tie in certain historical themes of the area of things like that and we are considering things of that sort."

In 1963, Walt began efforts through his company, WED Enterprises, to develop as his next project, a theme park in Florida, sparking an intense personal battle with Roy, who felt his pursuit represented a potential conflict of interest between his personally owned company and the stockholder-owned Walt Disney Productions. Biographer Bob Thomas wrote that "For months they would not talk to each other, communicating through intermediaries and impersonal memos. Only their close associates were aware of the frost between them" until they mended their fences.

Two years later, Walt purchased land in Orlando, a central Florida suburb, for the development of his so-called Florida Project. On an area twice the size of Manhattan Island, he planned to include a theme park like Disneyland but on a much larger scale: Disney World and Experimental Prototype Community of Tomorrow, better known as EPCOT. Involved throughout in the project's planning and development, by 1966, Walt established a design for EPCOT as "a high-technology, functioning community." He traveled throughout the United States to inspect cities in order to generate new ideas for EPCOT. Surrounding his Florida Project would be a "new kind of city" for its residents, utilizing the "best thinking about transportation, communication, and sanitation." As John Hench, who started with the studio in 1939 as a story artist and who had joined Walt's WED Enterprises, later said, "Solving the problems of the city obsessed him."

On November 15, 1965, at the Cherry Plaza Hotel in Orlando, after burying their differences, Walt and Roy made it official. Along with Florida Governor Haydon Burns, they made their first public announcements of plans to build the new Disney World Resort, near Orlando (the park would open five years after Walt's death).

Later that year, Walt embarked on a memorable 13-day yacht cruise with his wife, daughters, and their families through the waters of British Columbia. Resting and relaxing, he read books about city planning in making the dream of EPCOT exactly as he envisioned.

Between 1965 and 1966, Walt left his imprint on many other films he personally produced. Fittingly, they were a mix of lighthearted live-action comedies and dramas, including *Those Calloways; The Monkey's Uncle; That Darn Cat!* (based on the book *Undercover Cat* by Millie and Gordon Gordon); *The Ugly Dachshund; Lt. Robin Crusoe, U.S.N.; The Fighting Prince of Donegal;* and *Follow Me, Boys!*

On New Year's Day 1966, however, having celebrated his 64th birthday in December, his hair and neatly trimmed mustache a little grayer, Walt rode as the Grand Marshal in the Tournament of Roses Parade, watched by millions of viewers on television. Lillian and those around him noticed that his energy had begun to lag. He suffered from a host of health ailments, including a kidney ailment and aggravating pain in his left leg from his old polo injury, and often complained of feeling "pooped" and "gimpy" after the day's activities.

Friends rallied around him at dinner parties, telling the usually high-spirited, aging animator and filmmaker he would enjoy many years and many more parties. He bluntly told them with a smile, "No, I won't live forever."

Work and career still occupied his time, providing some solace. He continued hosting *Walt Disney's Wonderful World of Color* for NBC, made

A lifelong railroad enthusiast, Walt waves to onlookers as the chief engineer of the Disneyland Railroad in this photo taken in the mid-1960s. © *Disney.*

daily visits to his WED Enterprises office to view dailies of films in production, and worked on preproduction of two others, *The Happiest Millionaire* and *Jungle Book*, while overseeing the continued development of his Florida theme park project. His contributions to the cinematic arts, meanwhile, were celebrated on October 1, 1966, when the National Association of Theatre Owners made him their first award honoree as "Showman of the World."

A month later, on November 2, complaining of shortness of breath and pain in his left leg that was rendering it useless, Walt checked into St. Joseph Hospital in Burbank, which was in close proximity to the studio. Undergoing a battery of tests, X-rays revealed a dark spot—the size of a walnut—on his left lung. Doctors immediately suggested surgery, scheduled five days later on the following Monday.

Afterwards, Walt's surgeon discussed his prognosis with Lillian and his daughters Diane and Sharon. He had removed the cancerous left lung, but found Walt's lymph nodes were "oversized" and therefore he was unable to give them a positive outlook. He estimated Walt had six months to two years to live. They were stunned and had a difficult time fathoming the news.

Receiving good wishes from friends and fans around the world, Walt was released after two weeks in the hospital, regaining some of his vigor and cheerfully welcoming family visitors. Following his discharge, he insisted on returning to work. Looking considerably weak and drawn, many of his colleagues were shocked by his appearance. He worked on a variety of projects in development or in production.

After Thanksgiving, with cobalt treatments robbing him of his strength and appetite, Walt's health began to deteriorate. On November 30, upon returning from a trip to his Palm Springs retreat at Smoke Tree Ranch, he collapsed. Revived by medics, he was readmitted to St. Joseph Hospital. He never recovered. Two weeks later, on December 15, he breathed his last. At 9:30 A.M., he was pronounced dead of acute circulatory collapse, caused by lung cancer, at age 65.

A day later, a private funeral service was held by Walt's immediate family at Little Church of the Flowers of Forest Lawn Memorial Park in nearby Glendale, California, where he was interred in the Great Mausoleum, and final resting place of many notable movie stars from Hollywood's golden age. The next day, Roy, with whom Walt had had his differences, announced to studio management and the Imagineering team that the company would continue to run according to Walt's

Many years later, Walt's star shines bright on the historic Hollywood Walk of Fame.

wishes, and Walt's first name would be added to the title of the Florida theme park, now to be called, Walt Disney World.

As the flag flew at half mast at his famed Disneyland theme park, CBS News commentator Eric Sevareid, reflecting on the loss, said, "We'll never see his like again." In 1967, audiences would be treated to Walt's final films, *Monkeys, Go Home!*, a sequel to *The Misadventures of Merlin Jones* (in which The Beach Boys made their motion picture debut), *The Adventures of Bullwhip Griffin*, *The Gnome-Mobile*, *The Jungle Book*, and *The Happiest Millionaire*, reminding them of their loss as his studio struggled to move forward without his visionary talents.

Today, Walt Disney's legacy lives on. His monumental contributions to film and television, his enormous creativity and innovation, and his notable creations that have entertained millions remain as popular today. They continue to pay homage to the man whose impact on movies and the world will forever be felt and who roared his way into the record books because of his greatness and genius and a mouse named Mickey.

SELECTED RESOURCES

For further study of Walt Disney's work and career, the author recommends the following:

Filmographies

The Encyclopedia of Disney Animated Shorts (http://www.disneyshorts.org/years/1922/index.html)

This Web site covers all Disney cartoon shorts made from 1922 to the present, including release dates, running times, plot summaries, and more.

Walt Disney Filmography (http://www.imdb.com/name/nm0000370/)

Offers a complete filmography of every film Disney made categorized by year and by category—producer, director, actor, and writer.

DVD and Video Collections

Walt: The Man Behind The Myth (Walt Disney Home Entertainment 2004)

Two-hour made-for-TV special on the life and work of Walt Disney, narrated by comedian Dick Van Dyke.

Walt Disney Treasures: Disneyland U.S.A. (Walt Disney Home Entertainment, 2001)

Film critic Leonard Maltin hosts this two-disc set of televised specials from the weekly one-hour program, *Disneyland*.

Walt Disney Treasures: The Adventures of Oswald the Lucky Rabbit (Walt Disney Home Entertainment, 2007)

Two-disc collection of 13 surviving silent *Oswald the Lucky Rabbit* shorts out of the 26 Disney made, along with a bonus: Leslie Iwerks's documentary *The Hand Behind the Mouse: The Ub Iwerks Story* (1999), chronicling the life of her famous grandfather and Walt's first animator.

Walt Disney Treasures: Your Host, Walt Disney (Walt Disney Home Entertainment, 2006)

This two-disc set covers Walt Disney's work as host of the weekly anthology series *Disneyland* (later called *Walt Disney Presents*, then *Walt Disney's Wonderful World of Color*), and includes other rarities and extras.

SELECTED
BIBLIOGRAPHY

Adamakos, Peter. "Ub Iwerks." *Mindrot* (June 15, 1977).

Ballantine, Bill. "The Wonderful World of Walt Disney." *Vista II* (Winter 1966–67): 30–32.

Barrier, Michael. *The Animated Man: A Life of Walt Disney*. Berkeley: University of California Press, 2007.

———. "Building a Better Mouse: Fifty Years of Disney Animation." *Funnyworld*, No. 20 (Summer 1979).

Beck, Jerry. *The Animated Movie Guide*. Chicago: Chicago Review Press, 2005.

Canemaker, John. "Disney Design 1928–1979: How the Disney Studio Changed the Look of the Animated Cartoon." *Millimeter* (February 1979).

Davidson, Bill. "The Fantastic Walt Disney." *Saturday Evening Post* (November 7, 1964): 66–68, 71–75.

DeMille, Cecil B. "Interview: Walt Disney." Lux Radio Theatre, CBS. December 26, 1938.

Disney, Walt. "Walt Disney Employee Speech." Walt Disney Archives. 1941.

Eddy, Don. "The Amazing Secret of Walt Disney." *The American Magazine* (August 2, 1955): 29, 110–15.

Edera, Bruno. *Full Length Animated Feature Films*. New York: Hastings House, 1977.

Edson, Lee. "A Visit with Walt Disney." *Think* (May 1959): 25–27.

Gabler, Neal. *Walt Disney: The Triumph of the American Imagination*. New York: Vintage, 2007.

"Interview by David Griffiths." Walt Disney Archives. 1959.

"Interview with Hooper Fowler." *Look*. January 1964.

"Interview with Fletcher Markle." *Telescope*, Canadian Broadcasting Corporation. September 25, 1963.

"Interview by Tony Thomas." *Voices from the Hollywood Past*. Walt Disney Archives. 1959.

Jackson, Kathy Merlock. *Walt Disney: Conversations*. Jackson, Miss.: University Press of Mississippi, 2006.

Kent, George. "Snow White's Daddy." *Family Circle*, vol. 12, no. 25 (June 24, 1938): 10–11, 16.

Kinney, Jack. *Walt Disney and Assorted Other Characters*. New York: Harmony Books, 1988.

Lenburg, Jeff. *The Encyclopedia of Animated Cartoons, Third Edition*. New York: Facts On File, 2009.

Maltin, Leonard. *The Disney Films*. New York: Crown Publishers, 1984.

"Mr. and Mrs. Disney." *Ladies Home Journal* (March 1941): 20, 141.

Molloy, Paul. "Walt Disney: World's Most Successful Showman." *Success Unlimited IV* (September 1957): 4–7, 26.

Muir, Florabel. "How Silly Symphonies and Mickey Mouse Hit the Up Grade." *New York Sunday News* (December 1, 1929).

Nugent, Frank. "That Million-Dollar Mouse." *The New York Times Magazine* (September 21, 1947): 22, 60.

Rasky, Frank. "80 Million a Year from Fantasy." *Star Weekly* (Toronto) (November 14, 1964): 8–11.

Schickel, Richard. *The Disney Version: The Life, Times, Art and Commerce of Walt Disney*. New York: Simon and Schuster, 1985.

Shull, Michael S. and David E. Wilt. *Doing Their Bit: Wartime American Animated Short Films, 1939–1945*. Jefferson, N.C.: McFarland & Co., 1987.

Thomas, Bob. *Walt Disney: An American Original*. New York: Simon & Schuster, 1976.

"Walt Disney." *Authors and Artists for Young Adults*, Vol. 22 (1997).

"The Wide World of Walt Disney." *Newsweek* (December 31, 1962): 18, 49, 50.

Wiley, Mason and Damien Bona. *Inside Oscar: The Unofficial History of the Academy* Awards. New York: Ballantine Books, 1987.

INDEX

Page numbers in *italics* indicate photos or illustrations.

134

ABOUT THE AUTHOR

Photo courtesy: Brian Maurer.

Jeff Lenburg is an award-winning author, celebrity biographer, and nationally acknowledged expert on animated cartoons who has spent nearly three decades researching and writing about this lively art. He has written nearly 30 books—including such acclaimed histories of animation as *Who's Who in Animated Cartoons*, *The Great Cartoon Directors*, and four encyclopedias of animated cartoons. His books have been nominated for several awards, including the American Library Association's "Best Non-Fiction Award" and the Evangelical Christian Publishers Association's Gold Medallion Award for "Best Autobiography/Biography." He lives in Arizona.